TH

OF STORY

Global Myths on the Origins and
Character of Black people

To: Yvonne Young

From: Mary N. Muchiri
Muchiri... 9/11/13

MARY NYAMBURA
MUCHIRI (PH.D.)

Thank you for your support!

PublishAmerica
Baltimore

Hardcover 9781462662203
Softcover 9781462683758
PUBLISHED BY PUBLISHAMERICA, LLLP
www.publishamerica.com
Baltimore

Printed in the United States of America

Dedication

This book is dedicated to all, throughout all generations, who have suffered humiliation, exploitation and discrimination of all kinds, on account of the color of their skins.

You are loved by God, and he did not create you for this, but that you would show forth his glory. Do not let the man made story about your inferiority deprive you of your God given dignity and destiny.

Acknowledgements

I want to thank all who inspired me as I was writing, especially the stories that I have reproduced to illustrate my points.

Then there are those who read the manuscript and gave me suggestions. Among these were the members of the Grant County, Indiana, chapter of the American Christian Writers (ACW), Dr. Paul Rothrock, of Taylor University, who helped me check some of the scientific concepts, and Dr. Dennis Hensley, also of Taylor University, who made useful suggestions.

However, if there are still errors in the work, it is all my responsibility, not that of my readers.

Finally, I want to thank my husband, Humphrey Muciiri, to whom I went every time I was confused or needed to confirm any idea. My son, Timothy Muciiri, also helped to contribute some ideas on the design of the cover of this book.

To all I say, thank you and God bless you as you continue to inspire others as you did to me.

CONTENTS

CHAPTER 1

Introduction: An Example of a Powerful Story.

Have you ever wondered how people came to have different skin colors? Were they initially white, yellow or black? How did some races come to be thought of as superior and others inferior? How are you related to rocks, animals and plants, as well as other created things in the "chain of being?" Has Africa always been "The Dark Continent? Are these views based on facts or fiction?" These are the questions I shall try to answer in the pages that follow.

According to Bergman, "The Origin of Creation Myths,"

Almost every culture has a creation myth. On Biblical creation presuppositions, they are all basically variations of the core theme of the God-given creation account found in Genesis. A number of researchers have concluded that the source of all creation myths stems back to a common point, probably actual historical events in history (Van Over 1980; Roth, 1981). They all come from one early source and are different only because time and local cultural circumstances have embellished or altered them. This is the reason why the details in the creation myths vary, but either the basic outline is similar, or at least they share common elements.

Van Over, one of the leading "creation myth" researchers concluded (1980: 10), "The surprising and perplexing fact is that the basic themes for (creation) myths in widely different geographical areas are strikingly similar." Furthermore, these basic themes are contained in the record found in the second chapter of Genesis. This similarity has intrigued scholars for years. Rooth, (1981) analyzed 300 North American Indian creation myths and found that, aside from variations according to culture and other factors, the entire group had only a few basic themes.

As Van Over (1980:11) asks, "Why such similarity of mythic ideas and images throughout these distant cultures?" Many scholars have puzzled over this phenomenon; among them is the renowned Claude Levi-Strauss (1963: 208) who, after years of studying myths, says there is an "astounding similarity between myths collected in widely different regions (of the world)" and that "throughout (creation) myths resemble one another to an extraordinary degree." (Quoted in Van Over, 1980:11) Another eminent researcher, Kluckhohn (1965:168), concluded that "there is an outstanding similarity between myths collected in widely different regions." Regarding this similarity Van Over (1980: 11) concludes, "The scholarly argument has raged for decades and it continues to this day. No definite answer seems yet to have developed, but theories abound."

I started my personal search on the topic of myths when the truth of the following words resonated with me, as I read about the genocide in Ruanda. "Mixed up people learn a set of patterns and habits, among them the ability to name the demonic power of tribal loyalty. While many Western Christians can see the truth of this, they immediately think about Africa when they hear "*tribe, failing to realize that this is a spell that binds them.*" *My emphasis.* (Katongole, 2009)

This statement is in line with Keim's (1999,3), assertion of American ideas about Africa. "Ironically, even though we know little about Africa, we carry strong mental images about the continent...And although most Americans do not posses many facts about Africa, we do know certain general truths about the continent. We know, for example, that Africans live in tribes. And we know that Africa is a place of famine, disease, poverty, coups, and large wild animals."

My experiences in the US since 2001, when I moved to Indiana, seem to confirm the truth of these words. Many people have told me that these experiences are not typical of the whole US, but at the same time they represent the historical trend of the American nation.

America is a country of immigrants; yet, like the characters in George Orwell's *Animal Farm,* some have always been "more equal" than others. Moreover, the situation has become so normal that perhaps mainly because of my "resident alien" status, I am likely to have a different perspective. After all, the immigrants were supposed to be assimilated into speaking the English language, the symbol of a new America, whether they had come from Europe and spoke German or French or from Asia or Africa or were the original Indian natives of the country. They are acceptable now, as Americans, whereas I will be forever identified as an alien due to my "thick African accent."

Does such an accent exist? It only exists for those whose idea of Africa is that it is a country speaking one language. But those who know Africa are aware that it is a continent almost three times the size of the US where very many languages are spoken, with Kenya alone having 69, according to <ethnologue. com> on the languages of the world.

One thing that really puzzled me in the US was the difference between "race" and "ethnicity." How did one decide what was racial and what was ethnic identity? It appeared to me as if ethnicity was another word for "tribe," but only applicable to the minorities. The word also seemed to have a negative connotation for me. When I looked up the definitions of the two words in a dictionary, this was what I found:

Race: (ethnic group, nation, people, tribe, line)
Tribe: (ethnic group, family, clan, people)

My conclusion was that they mean the same, except that race is bigger; (nation), but not family or clan. How then can some members of the same nation be *"the nation"* while others, make up the clans and families? (Katongole, 51) seemed to be asking the same question about Rwanda.

Europeans and Americans love to use the language of tribes when speaking about Africa. Yet this language is unhelpful in understanding what is going on because it mystifies the reality of Africa…Does tribe have to do with size? Does it have to do with speaking a different language? Hutu and Tutsi speak the same language in Rwanda. So is tribe a label reserved for non-western people?

I really could not find a satisfactory answer to my question. (Katongole's, 52,) idea that *"we become the people we are because of the stories we tell ourselves,"* seemed to make sense. The Tutsis were told by their colonizers that they were superior to the Hutus, because the latter were the "Sons of Ham," Noah's son who was cursed by his father for not covering his nakedness. So they believed the story and repeated it to themselves until Hutus were ready to exterminate them during the 1994 genocide. *What stories have Americans been telling themselves that have produced the current situation, where blacks are seen as inferior, even after being freed from slavery, I wondered?* Or what *"old tapes"* have they been playing to themselves, as (Dolphus Weary, 73-81) wondered in his investigation of the topic, *"Do the men that beat us Worship the same God?"*

When I first came to the US I used to make fun of myself saying I had "the mark of Cain." I was speaking of a birthmark on the left side of my face. It had started as a small black patch, but grew to cover almost the whole left side of the face. My mother was convinced that I had been burned by a hot potato that she ate while pregnant with me. She had felt my movement as I tried to "run" from it. However, I can't vouch for the biological correctness of her experience.

Of course I was alluding to the Biblical story of the first man, Cain, who murdered his brother, Abel, and God put a mark on him as a punishment, (Genesis Chapter 4). He was cursed to wander in the wilderness and was afraid he would be killed, so God told him no one would kill him after he had the mark. So I said that I could not be a terrorist, since I had a mark that would identify me no matter where I went.

Later, I came to find out that this story had been used to explain how black people came into the world. The subject of the origins of black people fascinated me and the following chapters are about the myths that white people have used throughout the history of mankind to justify the dehumanization and enslavement of black people and the stereotypes that have developed as a result. *My hope is that both black and white people will see the folly and lack of any truth behind these myths, and decide to reject and expose these lies wherever they may still exist.*

I deal with three types of myths that are interrelated. *Section I* is about political systems that perpetuated racist ideologies. *Section II* illustrates how these myths originated as religious myths mainly based on misinterpretation of the Bible. *Section III* shows how all these myths were strengthened through pseudo-scientific claims based mainly on the theory of evolution and eugenics.

SECTION ONE: RACIST POLITICAL SYSTEMS

CHAPTER 2

Colonialism in Africa (1400-1900)

According to "How Europe Underdeveloped Africa" website:

> Colonialism refers to political and economic control by one state over another. The colonial experience began in the late 1400s, when Europeans arrived and set up trading posts in Africa. In the late 1800s and early 1900s European powers dominated many parts of the continent. Colonialism in Africa created nations and shaped their political, economic, and cultural development. The impact of colonialism is still being felt in the continent.
>
> Europeans sought to exploit the continent's economic resources. They therefore attempted to force African peoples to accept their rule. In the 1870s rival European nations colonized as much African territory as they could. By the late 1880s, they had divided up most of the continent among themselves in what has come to be known as "the scramble for Africa."

Christian missionaries were the first Europeans to establish churches in the interior of Africa. The missionaries facilitated the relationship between Africans and their colonizers, asking the Africans "to close their eyes in prayer while their brothers took the land," according to a popular Kenyan saying. However, Christian missionaries were also a disruptive force in African society since those Africans who converted to Christianity were required to radically reject their traditions. (See Muchiri, Naming Systems in Africa.) Some missionaries provided information to European armies and supported military expeditions against African groups that refused to accept Christianity.

Furthermore, European powers destroyed much of the political and social respect of traditional African chiefs and rulers without establishing lasting replacements for these authorities. The following quote from a Roman Catholic Missionary, clearly demonstrates the inferior attitude held against the language, culture and wisdom of the local people. Speaking of the Agikuyu (a Bantu group) of Kenya he says:

> Out of the darkness of this age old paganism that we have been studying, there are occasional gleams of natural intelligence to make the records of primitive life less repulsive. The inherited wisdom of the Kikuyu (the English version of the same group) is best revealed in his language, proverbs, legends, and fables. The Akikuyu do not possess books on ethics, psychology or other high-flown theories of modern science; but they possess a rich inheritance of common-sense which is handed down in oral tradition from father to son,...in the form of endless proverbs, parables and stories...(quotations) of which will almost certainly give some of our readers a pleasant surprise, accustomed as they are to hear the poor Africans described by the depreciatory appellation of "Black Devils," (Cagnolo, 213.)

It is interesting to compare this view of the African people with that of an administrator, who seems to find them much more intelligent and worth of recognition than the "man of God."

The inhabitants are a quick-witted, progressive and intelligent people, destined to play a prominent part in the development of Kenya. It follows that a knowledge of their customs and thoughts is indispensable to the Governmet Official, to the Missionary and in fact to all who come into close contact with them. (Cagnolo, Introduction by S.H. La Fontaine.)

Moreover, European colonialism introduced Africans to various aspects of Western culture meant to divide them. So after political independence, the colonies became African nations consisting of diverse groups with little in common with their fellow citizens. For example, African schools and universities were based on European systems of education and religion, yet they did not often deal with issues that were relevant to the African people. Moreover, African Christians were never equal to their white "brothers," especially in leadership.

The continent came to be known as the "Dark Continent" and its black peoples as inferior to the white colonizers. Keim (1999, 4) gives us three reasons why this came about.

He starts by saying that; "Anyone who wants to study Africa in depth needs to learn an African language, because language is a major key to understanding how people mentally organize the world around them." One would think Americans and Europeans would understand that, since wherever they went they took their English language. But Africa was different; it was there to be exploited not to be understood. As (Keim, 4) explains, "This exploitation of Africa, whether direct or indirect, required thinking about Africans as inferiors. In other words our (American) culture has had a lot of practice, hundreds of years of it, in constructing Africa as inferior."

The second reason he gives is that the stereotypes that were invented have persisted over time. "Africa became representative of extreme "otherness…Africa certainly became a primary symbol that Europeans and white Americans used to express difference…that has meant that the continent has been treated as an object…Africans cannot speak for themselves or make comments on who we are." (10-11) For example, I have discovered that an American who goes to Africa for two weeks is usually regarded as more of an expert than an African who was born and lived there for more than fifty years or more. This has happened even in my own institution!

The third reason (Keim, 23) gives is that "they tended to make Africans look like the Africa they imagined rather than the one that existed." He quotes a study of college graduates in which respondents commonly used words such as tribe (90%), primitive (69%), cannibals (60%) and savages (60%). These are words that were popularized by media. I have noticed the same trend among my students. When they want to contrast America with other countries for such things as corruption or poverty, Africa is the first to be mentioned. Most times it is treated as a country, with a homogenous culture rather than a continent with many countries and cultures.

Two examples will help to illustrate this point. In the mid-1990s, AT&T published an internal newsletter with a map of the world depicting its global telephone network. On each continent there was a person in local dress talking on a telephone connected to other continents via wireless and telephone poles. In Africa, however, there was a **chimpanzee** talking on the phone. After objections, the artists apologized, stating that they meant no harm and were just trying to add interest to their drawing.

As recently as 2011, a similar thing happened. A "Christian woman," representative Davenport, circulated an e-mail with President Obama pictured as a child of two chimpanzees. It was a time when many republicans were suggesting that he was born in Africa, not in Hawaii, and that he did not have a genuine birth certificate.

Californian Republican has apologized for an email that she sent to "friends and acquaintances" of President Barak Obama's face imposed as a chimp.

Tea Party activist, Marilyn Davenport, who represents the 72nd Assembly District in Orange County, sent a picture via email of three chimps; two being the parents and the third being the president as a child, with the tagline "Now you know why no birth certificate."

Scott Baugh, the chairman of the Republican Party of Orange County, released a statement saying he plans to investigate the incident. Baugh also calls for Davenport resignation saying the email was "highly inappropriate... it's a despicable message, it drips with racism, and I think she should step down from the committee."

Upon hearing what Baugh had to say—Davenport says that she has no plans to resign. (Davenport).

If that is not racist, as some have suggested, I do not know what is! It certainly reminds one of "Dark Africa" where humans are supposed to intermarry with monkeys.

These views of Africa apparently did not exist before 1400s, since before that Africa was an equal contributor to the Greek and Roman civilizations. For example (Oden, 158-197) *How Africa Shaped the Christian Mind,* lists many examples of Africans starting from the first century to the present who significantly contributed to the spread of Christianity. The better known names include Simon of Cyrene, Mark and Clement in Alexandria, Tertullian of Carthage, and Saint Augustine of Hippo, to name a few. I believe if these were just chimps we would not be reading about their work today. Contrary to the thinking of people like Marilyn Davenport, these were intelligent people whose ideas have influenced the lives of many in a positive way. For example, Saint Augustine is credited with starting the monastic orders that spread to Europe and many other parts of the world and continue even today.

For example, Augustinians of the Province of St. Thomas are involved in parish ministry, the educational apostolate and several other ministries, many focused on people on the fringes of society. Additionally, friars from the province serve in foreign missions in Japan, Peru and South Africa. In many specialized ministries and in their mission work, the friars work with lay women and men committed to the values the Augustinians promote. <http://www.augustinian.org/home>

However, when colonialism started, the Europeans *"felt the need to justify their actions in moral terms."* After all they were Christians behaving like the pagans they were supposed to convert! A racist theology came in handy. Consequently, "most of our modern stereotypes about Africa are a result of the nineteenth and twentieth century associations of the African race with African culture." The type of racism that resulted from this association has been described as "moderate racism" which "condemned individual Africans as bad men-or all Africans as savage men-but left the impression that *Africans* **were** men" (Keim, 30). However, to justify the enslavement of one man made in the image of God by another needed a new type of rationalization that will be discussed in the next chapter.

CHAPTER 3

Slavery (1500-1900)

It is obvious that not every white person agreed with the idea of enslaving Africans, as the following statement suggests: Proslavery and antislavery activists alike were racist, but both assumed that cultural factors were at the heart of the slavery question. For proslavery proponents, the Africans' inferior culture justified the institution. Antislavery activists argued that Christian charity required abolition and that Africans had the potential to acquire civilized culture. And there was the economic issue for both sides: slavery tended to be supported by those who benefited from it and abolition by those who would benefit from its end.

In what Keim calls "a myth of conquest, Africa is constructed as the Dark Continent, full of savages and barbarians." As recently as 2005, a former British soldier, commenting on my book <u>Saved Through Fire...</u>in a Taylor student paper, the Echo, said that as a Mugikuyu (a member of a Bantu people group in Kenya), "I had nothing to be proud of" considering the barbaric way in which we treaded not only the white people, but those from other people groups during Kenya's war of independence. A student of mine responded to him reminding him that the British colonizers were some of the most barbaric people in history. Barbarism is portrayed as belonging to certain cultures, rather than associated with an individual person's behavior.

In her article on "A 'Civilizing' Mission in Late Colonial Kenya" Caroline Elkins makes the comment that, "On the dreadful balance sheet, the murders by Mau Mau adherents were quite small in number compared with those committed by the British." (Chronicle of Higher Education B9 of January 21, 2005.) In the same article she adds, "Mau Mau (Kenya's Liberation Movement) was portrayed as a barbaric, anti-European, and anti- Christian sect that had reverted to tactics of primitive terror to interrupt the British civilizing in Kenya...The battlefield was...a vast system of detention camps where colonial officials reportedly held some 80,000 Kikuyu insurgents." She however discovered that many documents were missing and that the actual number of detainees was closer to 300.000, and there had been a campaign to eliminate the Kikuyu people. I know a saying that developed at the time among colonial administrators that **"The only good Kikuyu is a dead one."**

As Rudyard Kipling explains, it becomes the "White Man's Burden" to control the natives. "The colonial burden is no longer a call from God to convert the pagans, but from "whiteness," as the following verse of his poem illustrates, (Keim, 37)

Take up the White Man's burden
Send forth the best ye breed-
Go bind your sons to exile

To serve your captives' need;
To wait in heavy harness,
On fluttered folk and wild-
Your new-caught sullen peoples,
Half devil and half- child.

The more different the people were from whites, the more devil-like and child like. Black people could not be treated as real humans and so it was morally right to enslave them. Patrick Brantlinger explains the connection between slavery and the constructed inferior African race as follows:

> The myth of the Dark Continent defined slavery as the offspring of tribal savagery and portrayed white explorers and Missionaries as the leaders of a Christian crusade that would vanquish the forces of darkness…When the taint of slavery fused with sensational reports about cannibalism, witchcraft and apparently shameless sexual customs, Victorian Africa emerged draped in that pall of darkness that the Victorians themselves accepted as reality, (Keim, 36.)

Colonialism and slavery were supposed to be the most generous gifts to Africans. Perhaps they were; after all here I am writing in English, although I shall never write well enough, as I was recently reminded by my colleagues. However, they will never be required to learn my primitive language. African Americans who speak Ebonics, which is a dialect of English with some influence from African languages are also said to be speaking "broken English." It appears as if only by becoming white and speaking English will any black person become fully human- even in the 21st century.

As recently as 2005, during a workshop on the Trans-Atlantic Slave Trade, we were informed that if Africans had not been brought to America as slaves they would all have died of drought! I wonder how it is that there are people still surviving in Africa after the trade was abolished. It is also clear that the abolition was only possible when the trade ceased to be economically viable.

Speaking about the effects of slavery on both the whites and the slaves, (Booker T. Washington, 9) says:

> The harmful influences of the institution were not by any means confined to the Negro. This was fully illustrated by the life upon our own plantation. The whole machinery of slavery was so constructed as to cause labor, as a rule, to be looked upon as a barge of degradation, of inferiority... When freedom came, the slaves were as well fitted to begin life anew as the master, except in the matter of book-learning and ownership of property.
>
> The slave owner and his sons had mastered no special industry,...On the other hand, the slaves in many cases had mastered some hand craft and none were ashamed, and few were unwilling to labor.

More on the effects of slavery is discussed in chapters 13 and 14. Suffice it here to say that the issue of slavery confused many western Christians until its abolition. What a contradiction to the Biblical message of a savior who died for all people. However, even as late as 2009 during the Obama campaign for presidency, many of the old prejudices against black people were revived, and I understand hate speeches and crimes have increased since his election. Unfortunately, these are not limited to the KKK and other white extremists, but include many ordinary citizens such as those I encounter daily at work, shopping malls and restaurants.

Chapter 4

Apartheid (1600-1900)

According to http://countrystudies.us/south-africa/ website, Christianity became a powerful influence in South Africa, often uniting large numbers of people in a common faith. In the twentieth century, however, several Christian churches actively promoted racial divisions through the political philosophy of apartheid. The largest of these denominations was the Dutch Reformed Church (Nederduitse Gereformeerde Kerk—NGK), which came to be known as the "official religion" of the National Party during the apartheid era. Its four main branches had more than 3 million members in 1,263 congregations in the 1990s.

The Dutch Reformed Church arrived in South Africa in the seventeenth century, after Calvinist reforms in Europe had entrenched the idea of predestination, and the Synod of Dort in the Netherlands had proclaimed this church as the "community of the elect" in 1619. The church gained recognition as the state religion in 1651, and the Dutch East India Company, as an extension of the state in southern Africa, established the first Dutch Reformed Church at the Cape of Good Hope in 1652.

As black Africans and people of mixed race converted to the religion, church members debated the question of racial separation. Pressures grew for racially separate congregations, and the issue was complicated by the demands of some black church members for their own churches and congregations. In 1881 the Dutch Reformed Mission Church (Sending Kerk) established a separate colored church. In 1910, when black South Africans made up about 10 percent of the community, the synods established the NGK in Africa, as it became known, for black Africans. (An Indian Dutch Reformed Church was formed later in 1951.)

Racial separation was only widely accepted in the church in the early twentieth century, as many Afrikaners came to believe that their own survival as a community was threatened, and as the belief in racial separation was gaining acceptance among white South Africans in general. Social and spiritual survival became intertwined in church philosophy, influenced in part by the early twentieth-century persecution of the Afrikaners by the British (see British Imperialism and the Afrikaners). Church leaders refused to condemn Afrikaner rebellions against the British, and their followers gained strength by attributing divine origins to their struggle for survival.

As the system of apartheid was called into question throughout the country in the 1970s and the 1980s, church leaders were, in general, more committed to apartheid than many of their followers, and the church became an impediment to political reform. A few Dutch Reformed clergy opposed apartheid. The best known of these, Reverend Beyers Naude, left his whites-only church in the late 1970s and joined a black parish within the Dutch Reformed church. The efforts of other church leaders who worked to reduce the church's racist image were often constrained by the fact that parish finances were controlled by the church's highest authorities, who supported apartheid.

THE NATIONAL PARTY

According to http://www.english.emory.edu/Bahri/ apart.html website, the apartheid was a creation of three hundred and seventeen laws by Dr. D.F. Malan's nationalist party, which was elected in 1948. The apartheid only proceeded to add structure to the racial segregation and domination that already existed within the nation. Even before 1948, **the Nationalist Party feared the influx of Africans into White towns,** and therefore restricted the areas in which they could live. The Whites passed various bills in the next four decades, to ensure that the movements of Africans into their towns were kept at a minimum, and also sought political, economic, and social domination of the colored peoples.

According to another website on apartheid in South Africa, its operation among the people was almost like slavery:Apartheid was implemented by the law. The following restrictions were not (only) social but were strictly enforced by law. Non-whites were excluded from national government and were unable to vote except in elections for segregated bodies which had no power. Blacks were prohibited from holding many jobs and were not allowed to employ whites. Non-whites were not allowed to run businesses or professional practices in any areas designated as being for whites only. Every significant metropolis, practically every shopping and business district was in a white area. "Blacks (except for a few who had Section 10 rights), being in excess of 70% of the population, were excluded from all but a small proportion of the country, unless they had a pass which was impossible for most to get". Implementation of this policy resulted in the confiscation of property and the forced removal of millions of blacks. A pass was only issued to someone who had approved work; spouses and children had to be left behind. A pass was issued for one magisterial district, confining the (black) holder to that area only. "Being without a valid pass made a black person subject to immediate arrest, summary trial and deportation to the homeland. Police vans containing sjambok-wielding officers roamed the white area to round up the illegal blacks."

The land assigned to blacks was typically very poor, unable to support the population forced onto it. Black areas rarely had plumbing or electricity. Hospitals were segregated, the white hospitals being the match of any in the western world, the black ones being comparatively seriously understaffed and underfunded and far too few in numbers. Ambulances were segregated, forcing the race of the person to be correctly identified when the ambulance was called. A "white" ambulance would not take a black to a hospital. "Black" ambulances typically contained little or no medical equipment.

In the 1970s each black child's education cost the state only a tenth of each white child's. Higher education was practically impossible for most blacks: South Africa's few world class universities were reserved for whites. Besides, the schooling provided for blacks was deliberately not designed to prepare them for university but for the menial jobs available to them.

Trains and buses were segregated. White trains also had no third class carriages, while black trains were overcrowded and had only third class carriages. Black buses stopped at black bus stops and white buses at white ones.

Beaches were racially segregated, with the majority (including all of the best ones) reserved for whites. Public swimming pools and libraries were racially segregated but there were practically no black pools or black libraries.

There were almost no parks, cinemas, sports fields or any amenities except police stations in black areas. Park benches were all labeled "Europeans Only". Sex between the races was prohibited. Black policemen were not allowed to arrest whites. Blacks were not allowed to buy most alcoholic beverages. A black could be subject to the death penalty for raping a white, but a white raping a black faced only a fine, and often not even that. Cinemas in white areas were not allowed to admit blacks. Restaurants and hotels were not allowed to admit blacks, except as staff.

Membership in trade unions was not allowed for blacks until the 1980s, and any "political" trade union was banned. Strikes were banned and severely repressed. The minimum yearly taxable income for blacks was 360 rand (30 rand a month), while the white threshold was much higher, at 750 rand (62.5 rand per month). Apartheid pervaded South African culture, as well as the law. "A white entering a shop would be served first, ahead of blacks already in the queue, irrespective of age, dress, or any other factors. Until the 1980s, blacks were always expected to step off the pavement to make way for any white pedestrian. A white boy would be referred to as 'Klein Baas' (little boss) by a black; a grown black man would be addressed as 'Boy' by whites."

THE FIGHT FOR RACIAL EQUALITY

Religious alliances provided a means of coordinating church opposition to apartheid while minimizing the public exposure of church leaders and parishioners. The South African Council of Churches (SACC) was the most active antiapartheid umbrella organization. The SACC not only opposed apartheid but also offered encouragement to those who contravened race laws. Under the leadership of Anglican

Archbishop, Desmond Tutu, in the 1980s, the SACC also attempted to withhold cooperation with the state, as much as possible, in protest against apartheid. SACC leaders were outspoken in their political views, lodging frequent complaints with government officials and organizing numerous peaceful protests.

Countering the efforts of the antiapartheid community, the Christian League of Southern Africa rallied in support of the government's apartheid policies. The Christian League consisted of members of Dutch Reformed and other churches who **believed apartheid could be justified on religious grounds.** The group won little popular support, however, and was criticized both for its principles and for its tactic of bringing religious and political issues together in the same debate

Nelson Mandela became involved with the African National Congress, ANC, during the peak of the Second World War. Along with sixty other members, the mission of the ANC was to turn the group into a mass movement. By 1952, Mandela was elected National Volunteer-in-Chief. His job was to travel around the country, organizing resistance against discrimination. Because of his role in the ANC, Mandela was convicted of going against the Suppression of Communism Act and sent to Johannesburg prison for six months. After the Sharpeville Massacre in 1960, the ANC was outlawed. Mandela continued to fight for the rights of his people, traveling illegally outside South Africa in 1962, and addressing the Conference of the Pan African Freedom Movement of East and Central Africa. After his return to South Africa, he was once again arrested and sentenced to five years in prison. During these five years, he was charged with sabotage, and sentenced this time to life in prison. Like Gandhi and Martin

Luther King Jr., Mandela fought a war of non-violence and equal opportunities for all the people of South Africa. He was released on February 11th, 1990, and was elected as the first democratically chosen president of South Africa on May 10th 1994. In 1993, he received the Nobel Peace prize on behalf of all the South Africans who suffered to bring peace to the land.

According to a website on Africans and industrialization, the reasons for Apartheid were very similar to those for colonialism and slavery, mainly to divide the people so that they can be controlled to provide cheap labor.

Mine owners argued that if they did not get cheap labor their industries would become unprofitable. White farmers, English- and Dutch-speaking alike, interested in expanding their own production for new urban markets could not compete with the wages paid at the mines and demanded that blacks be forced to work for them. They argued that if blacks had to pay taxes in cash and that if most of their lands were confiscated, then they would have to seek work on the terms that white employers chose to offer. As a result of such pressures, the British fought wars against the Zulu, the Griqua, the Tswana, the Xhosa, the Pedi, and the Sotho, conquering all but the last. By the middle of the 1880s, the majority of the black African population of South Africa that had still been independent in 1870 had been defeated, the bulk of their lands had been confiscated and given to white settlers, and taxes had been imposed on the people, who were now forced to live on rural "locations." In order to acquire food to survive and to earn cash to pay taxes, blacks now had to migrate to work on the farms, in the mines, and in the towns of newly industrialized South Africa.

The same tactics were employed for colonial subjects as well as slaves. They were based on color differences and the idea that these people were also biologically, mentally, intellectually and culturally inferior to the superior white man. These included:

- Division of the family unit
- Confiscation of land
- Imposition of taxes
- A new identity based on servitude.
- Disruption of all their cultural values.

CHAPTER 5

Nazism (1800-2010)

Today, many anti-Semite and similar racist movements draw their inspiration from "Social Darwinism." In the manifesto of one of the most radical racist organizations in the US, the National Alliance, the bases of this doctrine are clearly set out.

The National Alliance organization stresses the difference between it and "Semitic beliefs" (Islam, Christianity and Judaism), and states that they believe only in nature, that they are "evolutionists," whereas "Semitic beliefs" are based on faith in God. In the manifesto, the evolutionist logic behind its racist ideology is described as follows:

> Our world is hierarchical. Each of us is a member of the Aryan (or European) race, which, like the other races, developed its special characteristics over many thousands of years during which natural selection not only adapted it to its environment but also advanced it along its evolutionary path. Those races which evolved in the more demanding environment of the North, where surviving a winter required planning and self-discipline, advanced more

rapidly in the development of the higher mental faculties. (Racism and Social Darwinism.)

The National Alliance Organization is based in the United States and produces books and magazines in Swedish, French, German, Portuguese and Russian. It is rapidly spreading its Darwinist, neo-pagan ideology, **"Cosmotheism,"** a racist religion that stresses "the superiority of the white race and the unity of the white race with nature." The articles inside the organization's fascist <u>National Vanguard</u> magazine frequently quote from the works of Darwin and other ideologues of Social Darwinism. One can find similar statements, Darwinist comments, and propaganda defending deviant pagan culture against the divine religions in the publications and web sites of other fascist organizations.

Put briefly, fascist racism, which was born with the re-awakening of pagan culture and the theory of naturalistic evolution in the 19th century, continues to grow in the 21st century, based on the same fundamental notions- **"a mono racial state, devoid of all foreign influences,"** according to the <u>National Vanguard </u># 139 of August 2007. Also according to #137 of April 2007, even the Confederate Army was wrong in using "Nonwhite soldiers and support staff."

An illustration from the 19th century reflects the racist aspirations of its time. A black person is on the same tree with a chimp, a gorilla and an orangutan.(Racism and Social Darwinism website) This hatred and disdain for colored people were important elements of the Nazi ideology that are still evident today among those who are anti-Semitic and anti black, like the Klu Klax Klan, and other hate groups.

A website about the Klu Klax Klan has the following description of the clan members:

At first, the Ku Klux Klan focused its anger and violence on African-Americans, on white Americans who stood up for them, and against the federal government which supported their rights. Subsequent incarnations of the Klan, which typically emerged in times of rapid social change, added more categories to its enemies list, including Jews, Catholics (less so after the 1970s), homosexuals, and different groups of immigrants.

I remember reading about a case of a man who had stubbed an African American woman at the back, just because she was black, in Kokomo, Indiana, many years before I came to the US. Then he had recently been handed over to the police by his own daughter, who was in the car when that happened, but was afraid to speak about it. She told the police that it had been such a burden of guilt to her that she finally decided to give her father up. When he was arrested and convicted, he committed suicide, rather than be jailed for "murdering a nigger."

According to the Southern Poverty Law Center, hate groups in the US topped 1,000 in 2010. They said they counted 1,002 active hate groups in the United States in 2010. Only organizations and their chapters known to be active during 2010 were included. All hate groups have beliefs or practices that attack or malign an entire class of people, typically for their immutable characteristics.

The following "joke," which was the least offensive, was found in the kkkomedy website: accessed on 12/22/2011. All the jokes are about the ugliness, immorality and disgusting actions of black people, as compared to the beauty, moral uprightness and good actions of white people.

A Nigger lady gets on a bus with her baby and puts the bus fee in the cup. The bus driver looks at the lady and says "that is the ugliest baby i have ever seen!" The Nigger gets mad and storms to the back of the bus and sits down. She then tells the man beside her "the bus driver just insulted me and i am very offended!" The man replies, "you shouldnt take that, go give him a piece of your mind!" The Nigger says, "you know, i think i will." Then the man says, "you go give him a piece of your mind, i'll hold your monkey."

SECTION TWO:
RELIGIOUS
MYTHS BASED ON
MISINTERPRETATION
OF THE BIBLE

Chapter 6

The Two Creations

We now know there is a racial problem, but how did it come about? I did some further reading to try and find out how the whole idea was introduced to black people, and the processes through which the story was repeated long enough to convince them that they were inferior to white people. I found out, to my great surprise, that many of the myths were based on the misinterpretation of the Bible.

While societies still cannot agree on how humans came to be here, whether due to the Big Bang, the process of evolution or according to the Genesis story of creation, none of these explain how some people became white and others brown or even black, if we all came from the same source. People all over the world have their own stories of their origins as well. For example, my people, the *Agikuyu of Kenya,* tell their children the story of their parents, Gikuyu and Mumbi, and how they prayed for children and were given nine girls (mothers of the clans), and then they prayed for sons and were given nine men who married the girls. The race *(ruriri)* continued to grow as they moved and multiplied.

According to (Jordan, 3-43), and as we saw earlier from Keim, the main myths about black people arose as a result of the *"first impressions"* that the white people developed during their first contacts with black people in Africa. These were then used to rationalize their treatment of the black people as the "unknown other and then as their slaves in the new lands they were discovering, especially America." One thing that makes this view credible is a comparison of the views about blacks in Brazil and in the US. In Brazil, blacks can "whiten" themselves through wealth, but that never happened in the US.

From the poem quoted from Degler, we see that the "kinky hair" has been associated with the idea that God could not have made the black man. He will not go to heaven because his hair "might stick Our Lord." The last line explains that, *"The Negro is the son of Satan."* Below is the full poem as quoted from Degler (114):

Negroes aren't born; they just appear.
Negroes don't marry; they just live together.
Negroes don't eat; they bolt their food.
Negroes don't dry themselves; they just shake the water off.
Negroes don't comb their hair; they curry it.
The Negro if he doesn't soil things on entering, soils them before he leaves.

The Negro was born to be a dog,
And to spend his life barking.
The Negro will not go to heaven,
Even though he prays,
Because his hair is kinky,

It might stick Our Lord.

The white man is a son of God,
The mulatto is a foster child
The *cabra* has no relatives
The Negro is a son of Satan.

The white man goes to heaven,
The mulatto stays on earth
The *caboclo* goes to Purgatory
The Negro goes to Hell

The white man sleeps in bed,
The mulatto in the hall,
The *caboclo* in the parlor,
The Negro in the "privy."

The question then arises as to how the myth originated. This will take us back to Genesis Chapters 1 & 2. In chapter one verses 26-27 we learn the following:

26. Then God said, let us make man in our image, in our likeness, and let them rule over the fish of the sea and the birds of the air, over the livestock, over all the earth, and over all the creatures that move along the ground.
27. So God created man in his own image, in the image of God he created him; male and female he created them.

Then in chapter two verse 4 and 7 we read:
4. This is the account of the heavens and the earth when they were created…

7. The Lord God formed the man from the dust of the ground
    and breathed into his nostrils the breath of life and the man
    became a living being.

The second question that arises is whether the second
chapter is describing the same or a different creation from that
in chapter one. The third is if both are by God or one is by
Satan, as the following folktale of Sao Paulo helps to clarify:
(Degler 116/7)

ORIGINS OF THE RACES

Long ago all men were black. One day God resolved to
reward the courage of each one without telling them; he
ordered them to cross a river. *The quickest and he who had
the most faith,* quickly carried out God's order, crossing the
river by swimming. When he emerged on the other side he
was completely *white, which was beautiful.*

The second when he saw what had happened to his
brother also ran to the waters of the river, doing the same
thing that he had done. But the water was dirty and he came
out on the other side only yellow.

The third also wanted to change color, imitating his
two brothers. But the water was much dirtier, and when he
arrived at the other side, he saw with disgust that he was
only a mulatto.

The fourth *was very sluggish and lazy,* when he arrived
at the river; God had already made it dry. Then he moistened
his feet and hands, pressing them over the river bed. It is in

this way that the black has only the palms of the hands and soles of the feet white, *and he is less than the others.*

A NORTHERN AMERICAN VERSION OF THE SAME STORY:

God, in order to finish the work of creating the world, made man and woman, who were placed in paradise. But the devil, during the completion of the work, was envious and jealous. He suggested that he was capable of creating the same prodigy. God, in order to *punish him* for such audacity, called him and ordered him to make another man.

Proudly the devil began the work, conscious of his power. Egoist! He *amassed the black clay*, in imitation of what God had done, and after hours and hours of work, completed a beautiful statue, equal to that of Adam.

He blew upon his work to give it movement, but *it remained black*; more black

Indeed than the original clay. What disillusionment! He pressed for a Dispensation in order to better the situation. To do this the artisan resolved to wash his man. He carried him to the edge of the river and began to wash him. He scrubbed and washed him so much that *the hair became kinky*, without, however, the skin getting lighter. Horrible!

He gave him a slap, a tremendous slap that knocked the figurine to the ground, *thickening the lips and flattening the nose*. More furious than ever, the unfortunate artisan took up his black figure and carried it to the beach. He attempted to drown it with a push that knocked it into the water. It must be destroyed! But the waters refused it and the black ended on all fours, with soles of his feet and palms of his hands in the wet sand.

Amazed, the devil then saw his creature get up. Unconcerned, *gay and happy, with a flat nose, large lips and kinky hair,* the soles of his feet and palms of his hands much lighter than the skin of his body. (The end of the story).

I think we need to ask a few questions about the two myths: Are they credible inferences from the Biblical story? Why are all the characteristics of the black person the opposite of what the white man considers "beautiful?"

My answer to whether there are two creations is a resounding "NO!" The so called two creations *are two summaries of the same action.* The first is a summary of the six days, while the second is a summary of the process of creating man. This is clear from the verses that follow: (verse 15/18)

The Lord God took the **man** and put **him** in the Garden of Eden to work it and take care of it… The Lord God said, "It is not good for **man** to be alone…"

There is nowhere we read about two men or two women. Moreover, the men who came up with the story had not merely a theological or aesthetic motive in condemning the black person's body and character, but a political and economic one too. Since many of the white men who went to Africa were either missionary or colonial officials from a Christian background, it was important that they were not understood to be abusing other human beings *"for whom Christ died."* They had to come up with a story to prove that these were savages at the level of animals.

Consequently, according to Jordan, because the Englishmen found the natives of Africa very different from themselves, they decided to equate them to apes. An example of the early descriptions of the African in 1563 is as follows:

> And entering in (a river) we see a number of black soules,
> Whose likeness seemed men to be, but all as black as coles.
> Their Captaine comes to me as naked as a naile,
> *Not having witte or honestie to cover once his taile,*
> *(Jordan 5).*

One is bound to ask, if Africans had tails in 1563, where did they go? Are there enough years for them to have evolved to the present condition? Or were they speaking *metaphorically* and those who read their descriptions took them literally? Of course, because they were different, they were also strange, and therefore, ugly. As Jordan explains, *these were their opposites!* (Jordan 7)

In England perhaps more than Southern Europe, the concept of blackness was loaded with intense meaning. Long before they found that some men were black, *Englishmen found in the idea of blackness a way of expressing some of their most ingrained values.*
No other color except white conveyed so much impact.

As described by the *Oxford English Dictionary,* the meaning of black before the sixteenth century included "Deeply stained with dirt; soiled, dirty, foul...Having dark or deadly purposes, malignant; pertaining to or involving death; deadly; baneful, disastrous. Sinister... Foul, iniquitous, atrocious, horrible, wicked...Indicating disgrace, censure, liability to punishment, etc."

Black was an emotionally partisan color, the hand maid and symbol of baseness and evil, a sign of danger and repulsion. Embedded in the concept of blackness was **its direct opposite-whiteness.** No other colors so *clearly implied opposition,* **"beinge coloures utterlye contrary"**; no others were used so frequently to denote polarization:

Everye white will have its blacke

And evrye sweete its sowre

White and black connoted purity and filthiness, virginity and sin, virtue and baseness, beauty and ugliness, beneficence and evil, **God and the devil.** (My emphasis)

Is it a wonder then that when the white man saw a black person he saw the **personification** of all that is evil? Moreover such a discovery was politically and economically beneficial because, as we mentioned in the discussion on colonialism and slavery, such a "devilish savage" would be easily conquered and exploited without causing any sense of guilt. It was a good foundation on which **to rationalize both colonization and slavery.**

It is therefore not difficult to see why black people would be associated with these evil traits of character since these concepts are still found in the English Language today, for example, *Encarta Dictionary*, gives the following meanings of black: "devoid of light", "funny and macabre", (black humor) "clandestine", "full of anger" (black mood) "hopeless" (a black future) "dirty", "bad or unfortunate" (a black day) "evil", "dishonorable"

Here is an example of how one of the early Roman Catholic Missionaries described the Kikuyu people of Kenya: (Cagnolo 20) "The Kikuyu temper is distrustful and suspicious with a tendency to dissimulation and guile: the usual barriers behind which the weak and inferior entrench themselves." This is very interesting, especially when compared to another description of the same people by Fontaine, an administrator, who wrote the introduction to Cagnolo's book: "The inhabitants are a quick-witted, progressive and intelligent people," as reported earlier.

CHAPTER 7

Mark of Cain

Once the creation of the black person was associated with Satan, a way had to be found to perpetuate the myth through all the human generations. So it is easy to see how blackness came to be connected with **Cain, the one "full of anger"**. Again we go back to genesis chapter 4:2b-7 where we read about the two brothers of the first family:

2b. Now Abel kept flocks, and Cain worked the soil.
3. In the course of time Cain brought some of the fruits of the soil as an offering to the Lord.
4. But Abel brought fat portions from some of the first born of his flock.
   The Lord looked with favor on Abel and his offering,
5. but on Cain and his offering he did not look with favor, so **Cain was very angry**, and his face was downcast.
6. Then the Lord said to Cain, "Why are you angry? Why is your face downcast?
7. If you do what is right, will you not be accepted? But if you do not do what is right, sin is crouching at your door, it desires to have you but you must master it."

The story continues to describe Cain's slippery slope from anger to jealousy to murder, to irreverence. Then in verse 11-16 God pronounces his judgment:

11. Now you are under a curse, and driven from the ground, which opened its mouth to receive your brother's blood…

13. Cain said to the Lord, "my punishment is more than I can bear…whoever finds me will kill me."

15b…**Then the lord put a mark on Cain**, so that no one who found him would kill him."

The ideas of a curse and a mark were both used to explain the connection between the creation of Satan and the continuation of the black people.

One example is from a recent article about The Mormon Church (the nickname for The Church of Jesus Christ of Latter-Day Saints), founded by the Prophet Joseph Smith in 1830, and headquartered in Salt Lake City, Utah, in the US, with a membership of over 13 million worldwide. It is also known as "The LDS Church". (Evenson)

The Curse of Cain Doctrine is an official doctrine of the LDS Church, taught by numerous Mormon prophets and apostles since 1848 until at least 1978. They taught that "Negroes" were "cursed" and "inferior" and "children of Cain" and that Cain was a white man until turned into the first "Negro" by the LORD after he had killed Abel. Then he married his sister who became the second "Negro" and all Negroes are the descendants of Cain and the *"Mark of Cain" was a black skin, flat nose, and kinky hair.*

The Curse of Cain was not supposed to end until after the Millennium (1000 year reign of Christ on earth); when Negro women would have white Caucasian children; a "sign" that the LORD had lifted the Curse of Cain off of the Negroes. <u>At no time</u> did Church leaders ever say that the Curse of Cain Doctrine was their "personal opinion" or "speculation". They *always* presented it as "Revelation" and called it "a doctrine of the Church" in several official statements by the First Presidency.

The Priesthood-Ban Policy is an official Church policy banning all Negroes and anyone with "one drop of Negro blood" from all Mormon temples and the Mormon priesthood; effectively assuring that anyone with Negro blood could not become Gods and Goddesses in the highest heaven; the goal of every faithful Mormon. Negroes could become Mormons, but were banned from the important Mormon Temple rites, and all priesthood offices. Every Mormon male over the age of 12 is supposed to hold the priesthood in some capacity.

The Curse of Cain Legacy is the Curse of Cain Doctrine and the Priesthood-ban Policy known collectively as "The Curse of Cain Legacy".

Mormon Temple Rites are a series of Masonic-like secret rituals in which faithful Mormons make covenants with the LORD. If Mormons keep (obey) these covenants, they are promised they will be appointed as Gods and Goddesses in the Afterlife; creating their own planets and begetting spirit-children to inhabit those planets, for all eternity. One rite is "Sealing" in which husbands are sealed to wives, and parents to children, for all eternity; thus creating "Eternal Families". Negroes and those with Negro blood were **banned** from these temple rites until 1978. Before 1978, **Black**

Mormons were promised they would become "servants" to white Mormons in the Celestial Kingdom should they remain faithful to the Church. (My emphasis)

On June 8th, 1978, Church President, Spencer W. Kimball, claimed to have ended the 130 year old Priesthood-ban policy, which was based completely on the Curse of Cain Doctrine. Most critics say that the **1978 Revelation** was due to mounting internal and external pressures upon the Church; such as the U.S. Government threatening sanctions against the Church unless it ended its discrimination against blacks. The 1978 Revelation, also called "Official Declaration 2" did not repudiate the Curse of Cain Doctrine nor call it a "mistake" *in any way.*

The Curse of Cain Cover-up is an unwritten policy of the LDS Church since at least 1996 in which all Church spokesmen are to deny that the Church ever taught the Curse of Cain Doctrine; calling it "speculation" and "folklore" and "never a doctrine of the Church" and then to state that the Church "doesn't know why" they banned blacks from the temples and priesthood for 130 years. All of these statements by LDS leaders and spokesmen are *lies* or *equivocations.* The Curse of Cain Cover-up is still going on today. Church leaders are doing what "The Party" did in George Orwell's book *1984*: **"The past was erased, the erasure was forgotten, the lie became the truth." (1984, p. 7)**

The Curse of Canaan Doctrine: Negroes are the descendants of Canaan (*son of Ham*), and under the "Curse of Canaan"; to be a "servant of servants" until the curse is removed. (Note: this doctrine was not taught by Mormon leaders after 1865).

Though I am not sure whether other churches taught the curse of Cain Doctrine, I am familiar with the idea of blacks as the **Sons of Ham.** However, before I discuss the Sons of Ham, I have to wonder why only blacks have to wait for the millennium to have the curse removed, if indeed they were cursed, while according to Galatians 3:13, "Christ redeemed us from the curse of the law by becoming a curse for us, for it is written: "Cursed is everyone who is hung on a tree." If this does not apply to blacks, then they are not people and so have no part in the kingdom of God, because Christ's work on the cross does not apply to them. That perhaps explains why slaves were regarded as **less** than human. It was not until *"After the war ended in 1865, (that) the Republican Congress passed the 13th Amendment abolishing slavery and the 14th Amendment providing full civil rights for all blacks, thus fulfilling the original promise of the Declaration of Independence,"* according to Free Republic website.

CHAPTER 8

The Sons of Ham

THE "CURSE OF CAIN" AND THE "CURSE OF HAM"

There is a distinction between the "curse" and the "mark" of Cain. The "curse of Cain" resulted in Cain being cut off from the presence of the Lord. The Genesis and Moses accounts both attest to this. The Book of Mormon teaches this principle in general when it speaks about those who keep the commandments will prosper in the land, while those who don't will be cut off from the presence of the Lord. This type of curse was applied to the *Lamanites* when they rejected the teachings of the prophets.

The exact nature of the "mark" of Cain, on the other hand, is unknown. The scriptures don't say specifically what it was, except that it was for Cain's protection, so that those finding him wouldn't slay him. Many people, both in and out of the Church, have assumed that the mark and the curse are the same thing, a black skin.

WHEN DID A BIBLICAL CURSE BECOME ASSOCIATED WITH THE "HAMITES?"

The origin of the "curse of Ham" pre-dates the establishment of the Church of Jesus Christ of Latter-day Saints by hundreds of years. The basis used is Genesis 9:18-27:

18.And the sons of Noah that went forth of the ark were Shem, and Ham, and Japheth: and *Ham is the father of Canaan.*

19.These are the three sons of Noah: and of them was the whole earthoverspread.

20.And Noah began to be a husbandman, and he planted a vineyard:

21.And he drank of the wine, and was drunken; and he was uncovered within his tent.

22.And Ham, the father of Canaan, saw the nakedness of his father, and told his two brethren without.

23.And Shem and Japheth took a garment, and laid it upon both their shoulders, and went backward, and covered the nakedness of their father; and their faces were backward, and they saw not their father's nakedness.

24.And Noah awoke from his wine, and knew what his younger son had done unto him.

25.And he said, *"Cursed be Canaan; a servant of servants shall he be unto his brethren."*

26.And he said, "Blessed be the Lord God of Shem; and *Canaan shall be his servant."*

27.God shall enlarge Japheth, and he shall dwell in the tents of Shem; and *Canaan shall be his servant.*

Genesis 9:18-27 (emphasis added)

According to the article: "Blacks and the priesthood/The 'curse of Cain' and 'curse of Ham,'" although these verses clearly state that Canaan is cursed, it is not clear that the curse would be extended to his descendants. The use of Genesis 9 to associate a biblical curse with the *descendants* of Ham actually began in the third and fourth centuries A.D. This "curse" became associated with the Canaanites. Origen, an early Christian scholar and theologian, makes reference to

Ham's "discolored posterity" and the "ignobility of the race he fathered." Likewise, Augustine and Ambrose of Milan speculated that the descendants of Ham carried a curse that was associated with a darkness of skin. This concept was shared among Jews, Muslims and Christians.

The first "racial justification" for slavery appeared in the fifteenth century in Spain and Portugal. In the American colonies, the "curse of Ham" was being used in the late 1600's to justify the practice of slavery. As author Stephen R. Haynes puts it, *"Noah's curse had become a stock weapon in the arsenal of slavery's apologists, and references to Genesis 9 appeared prominently in their publications."*

THE "MARK OF CAIN" WAS ASSOCIATED WITH BLACK SKIN BY PROTESTANTS TO JUSTIFY SLAVERY.

The idea that the "mark of Cain" and the "curse of Ham" was a black skin is something that was used by many Protestants as *a way to morally and biblically justify slavery.* This idea did not originate with Latter-day Saints, although the existence of the priesthood ban prior to 1978 tends to cause some people to assume that it was a Latter-day Saint concept.

Dr. Benjamin M. Palmer, pastor of the First Presbyterian Church in New Orleans from 1856 until 1902, was a "moving force" in the Southern Presbyterian church during that period. Palmer believed that the South's cause during the Civil War was supported by God. Palmer believed the Hebrew history supported the concept that God had intended for some people to be formed "apart from others" and placed in separate territories in order to *"prevent admixture of races."* Palmer claimed that, *"[t]he descendants of Ham, on the contrary, in whom the sensual and corporeal appetites predominate, are driven like an infected race beyond the deserts of Sahara, where under a glowing sky nature harmonized with their brutal and savage disposition." Palmer declared:*

Upon Ham was pronounced the doom of perpetual servitude—proclaimed with double emphasis, as it is twice repeated that he shall be the servant of Japheth and the servant of Shem. Accordingly, history records not a single example of any member of this group lifting itself, by any process of self-development, above the savage condition. *From first to last their mental and moral characteristics, together with the guidance of Providence, have marked them for servitude;* while their comparative advance in civilization and their participation in the blessings of salvation, have ever been suspended upon this decreed connexion [sic] with Japhet [sic] and with Shem.

Unfortunately, among some, the concept that God has separated people by race has persisted even into modern times.

God has separated people for His own purpose. He has erected barriers between the nations, not only land and sea barriers, but also ethnic, cultural, and language barriers. God has made people different one from another and intends those differences to remain. (Letter to James Landrith from Bob Jones University, 1998)

THE CURSE OF CANAAN
According to the article, "The Curse of Canaan," the grievous sin of Noah's son or grandson recounted in Genesis 9 has far-reaching implications, including slavery, as discussed below.

Some are of the opinion that the curse of Canaan involves racial superiority, and that the prophecy about Canaan (also a *ben* or son of Noah) being made a slave to his brothers and their descendants (vv. 25-27) directly condoned the enslavement of black people. This view was prevalent during the 18th-20th centuries even among Bible-believing Christians. *It was always assumed that Ham himself was a black man, however, only one of his sons, Cush, has a name meaning black.* The sons of Cush are widespread and his descendants are in Northeast and West Africa in both C and B Haplogroups, but they are also the ancestors of the HG C Australian Aboriginals (Hg. C4), some Indians but also the Mongols and some East Asians, Maori, Chippewa or Nadine, Cheyenne and Apache and the C3 element of the Maya Amerindians and the forebear of the black tribes of both Africa and India. It is probable that Ham's wife was also the mtDNA Haplogroup L, which is now confined to Africa (in L1 and L2). *Eve herself must have been red to dark-skinned, as was Adam.*

The possibility that our original parents may have been dark skinned is an interesting one. Perhaps instead of asking where black people came from, we should be asking how the white people came about. A close reading of Genesis chapter 10 "The Table of Nations" is not conclusive in suggesting that the people of Africa are the sons of ham and Canaan. It concludes with the words, "From these the nations spread out over the earth after the flood." Gen. 10:32)

CHAPTER 9

Tower of Babel and the Dispersion of the Nations

A THEORY IN RWANDA

In Rwanda, the Hamitic hypothesis was a racialist hypothesis created by John Hanning Speke, which stated that the "Hamitic" Tutsi people were superior to the "Bantu" Hutus because they were deemed to **be more "White" in their facial features, and thus destined to rule over the Hutus.**

The fact is that the Tutsis came in to Rwanda from the North East and were assumed to have Semitic lines from the Hebrew offshoots in Ethiopia. The Churches, both Roman Catholic and Anglican and even the Seventh-Day Adventists, actually compiled records on the Tutsis and then provided those records to the killing squads which they paid to engage in the massacres, and the nuns carried jerry cans of petrol to burn down the buildings in which the Tutsi victims took shelter. There were a number of bishops, ministers and nuns charged with genocide and other crimes, convicted and sent to prison for the offences. See a story contained in the web site <www.holocaustrevealed.org> published in the local newspaper, (*The New Times*, Kigali Rwanda, Issue No 211, 30 April- 3 May 2001-05-31 Front Page Article)

Bishop Musabyimana's indictment charges are that between April and May 1994, following the ethnic conflict in the then Gitarama prefecture, he (Musabyimana) publicly stated that the situation for the Tutsi was very bad and that their end had arrived. He is also accused of having instructed his subordinates to register, and group on ethnic basis, all refugees who had fled to Shyogwe Diocese, which lists were later used to isolate Tutsi refugees who were taken to nearby sites to be killed. The Bishop is also said to have paid the militias who carried out the killings.

The theory is part of a wider idea which returns us back to Genesis 11:1- 9, the story of the Tower of Babel.

1. Now the whole world had one language and a common speech.
2. As men moved eastward, they found a plain in Shinar and settled there.
3. They said to each other, "Come let's make bricks and bake them thoroughly." They used brick instead of stone, and bitumen for mortar.
4. Then they said, "Come let's build ourselves a city, with a tower that reaches to the heavens, so that we may make a name for ourselves and not be scattered over the face of the whole earth."
5. But the LORD came down to see the city and the tower that the men were building.
6. The LORD said, *"If as one people speaking the same language* they have begun to do this, then nothing they plan to do will be impossible for them.
7. Come, let us go down and confuse their language so they will not understand each other."

8. So the LORD scattered them from there over all the earth, and they stopped building the city.

9. That is why it was called Babel-because there the LORD confused the language of the whole world. *From there the LORD scattered them over the face of the whole earth.*

This story has generated many theories, including those that explain the black colour as a result of different types of climate, especially the hot climate of Africa. Black people are supposed to have more pigmentation to protect their skin from the hot sun. It is further argued that the hot climate is also responsible for their *laziness, and perhaps even their "mental retardation."*

Jordan cites one of the oldest Greek fables about Phaeton as a way of trying to explain blackness, (Jordan 11-13):

The AEthiopians then were white and fayre,
Though by the worlds combustion since made black
When wanton Phaeton overthrew the sun.

Jordan concludes, "In general, the most satisfactory answer to the problem was some sort of reference to the action of the sun, whether *the sun was assumed to have scorched the skin, drawn the bile or blackened the blood."* The interesting thing was that only those in Africa seemed to be affected in this way, but not others living in similar climates! Moreover those who were taken to colder climates did not get whiter. It was then concluded that blackness was the result of a disease.

In 1578,…a geographer, George best, announced,…"*it seemeth this blackness proceedeth rather of some natural infection* of that man, which was so strong, that neither the nature of the climate, neither the good complexion of the mother concurring, could anything alter, and therefore we cannot impute it to the nature of the climate."

Failing to get an adequate explanation, Christians were divided into two main groups. One group concluded *that blackness was as a result of "the heathen condition defined by negation of the proper Christian life."* A smaller group accounted blackness in the African "another manifestation of God's omnipotent providence." One example of the latter was Peter Heylyn in 1627.

The heathen condition was then extended to the whole character of the black person (the Negro), who could only attain *"savage nobility"* only by approximating the appearance of a white man. *He had to be treated as a beast, especially apes that shared his habitat.* An example of such a description is given by Jordan (30), where a British traveller describes the "apelike Negro" as follows:

> In addition to stressing the *"lustful disposition,"* of the *ape kind*, Topsell's Compilation contained suggestions concerning the character of simian facial features. *"Men that have low and flat nostrils,"...and having thick lips... they are deemed fooles, like the lips of asses and apes,"* (Jordan 30). (My emphasis)

The Bible is racially neutral and refers only to a curse on Canaan son of Ham for the actions that either Ham or Canaan perpetrated on Noah after the Flood.

According to the article, "Sons of Ham," there is only one name that has any indication of the term *colour*. Cush means *black*; Ham means *hot* or *multitude*. Yet, there are a number of nations of Cushite descent that are not black at all, but range from racially white to Asiatic, Polynesian or some of Amerindian descent. The YDNA groups are the only way some can be differentiated. The greatest man in ancient times was Nimrod, son of Cush, and it was he that established the cities of the Ancient Middle East (Gen. 10:6-11).

THE HAMITES
6. The sons of Ham
   Cush, Mizraim, Put and Canaan
7. The sons of Cush, Seba, Havilal, Sabtah, Raamah and Sabtecah
   The sons of Raamah: Sheba and dedan
8. Cush was the father of Nimrod who grew to be a mighty warrior…
15.Canaan was the father of Sidon…and of the Hittites…

The curse uttered by Noah against Canaan was carried out and the Canaanites were placed within the nations of both Shem and Japheth. **These were never known to have occupied Africa.**

These people—whose land was Palestine, to Tyre and Sidon, at present in Lebanon—were subjugated by and absorbed into the Hebrews and surrounding nations. They became slaves of slaves to false gods and were to be liberated in Christ.

Its (slavery) racist development in the USA is an indictment on the entire white civilisation there and in Britain. The year 2007 marks the bicentennial of the passing of a Parliamentary Bill to end Britain's involvement in the transatlantic slave trade, following protracted campaigns by William Wilberforce (1759-1833) and others. The Civil War saw the end of slavery in the US, but that was not the intention of the war.

At its height, the trade provided 40,000 African slaves a year for the British alone, while it has been calculated that about 28 million Africans in total were transported between 1450 and 1807. Three times as many were sent to the sugar plantations of Jamaica as to America.

A lesser-known fact is that Denmark, although only a minor player in the slave trade was actually the first country to legislate against it. This was followed by several of the northern American states. Most prominent among the British abolitionists were the humanitarian Quakers.

The Bible does not make any elevation in racial hierarchies but, in fact, proclaims that the Plan of God is to merge all nations into one people under the twelve Apostles as the twelve tribes of Israel; and all men are to be saved, as salvation is of the Gentiles through Jesus Christ.

As for the story of the Tower of Babel, there is no mention of color, all we are told is that the people are scattered because they could no longer communicate, as a result of the confusion of language. As a result, many different languages and cultures evolve as the people spread around the world.

Chapter 10

The Children of Lot

The story of Lot is another one based on a Biblical story. It is found in **Genesis chapter 19.** God decides to destroy Sodom and Gomorrah because of their wickedness. He sends two angels who are welcomed by Lot, Abraham's nephew. The men of the town hear of it and they demand that he gives them the men to have sex with them (they are homosexuals). Lot refuses and tries to give them his own virgin daughters, but they will not relent. The angels take over by making the men blind and telling Lot to go out of the city with all his relatives before the city is destroyed.

12. The two men said to Lot, "Do you have any one else here—sons-in-law, sons or daughters, or anyone else in the city who belongs to you? Get them out of here,
13. because we are going to destroy this place. The outcry to the Lord against its people is so great that he has sent us to destroy it."
14. So Lot went and spoke to his sons-in-law, who were pledged to marry his daughters. He said, "Hurry and get out of this place, because the Lord is about to destroy the city!" But his sons-in-law thought he was joking.

15. With the coming of dawn, the angels urged Lot, saying, "Hurry, take your wife and two daughters who are here or you will be swept away when the city is punished."
16. When he hesitated, the men grasped his hand and the hands of his wife and of his two daughters and led them safely out of the city, for the Lord was merciful to them…
26. But Lot's wife looked back and she became a pillar of salt.
27. Early the next morning Abraham got up and returned to the place where he had stood before the Lord.
28. He looked down towards Sodom and Gomorrah, towards all the land of the plain and he saw dense smoke rising from the land, like smoke from a furnace.
29. So when God destroyed the cities of the plain, he remembered Abraham, and he brought Lot out of the catastrophe that overthrew the cities where he had lived.

What does this have to do with black people, you may ask. I did not think it had either, until I came across the following story, in Jordan (242-3)

During the seventeenth century there had been little progress on the scientific problem of the Negro's blackness, and the reigning mood at the beginning of the eighteenth century was one of puzzlement, eclecticism and shotgun explanation. One popular writer disposed of the matter in the following illuminating manner:

Question: *What is the reason that some men are black and some are tawny, and some white, in the same climate, as in India?*

Answer: We shall endeavor a satisfaction by showing a diversity of Opinions about this matter, and by advancing an

Hypothesis of our own chargeable with as little absurdity as we can. Some have believed that Cain's mark was black, and therefore his Successor's Colour might be alter'd from what Adam's was, and so by new Marriages and Intermixtures the World might be diversely coloured.

Some say Lot's daughters, having upon their flight from Sodom, an Idea of the smoke and flames they left behind them, might very probably, in the act of Generation with their father, fix a similitude of Colour upon Conception, by the power of their imaginary faculty. Some that the nearness of distance of the Sun may have an Effect upon the Skin as the Portuguese are more tawny than the English, or Northern climates.

We shall give you one instance more and then lay down that we conceive to be the reason. One Mr. Briggins, now a Captain of a Privateer, who is yet alive, and may be heard of at the Tower, mentions in his journals, that they touched upon an island of Blacks [where the king]…told them that he had one Rarity in his Court, a white child born of his two Subjects, Blacks that had neither of them seen a white man or woman in all their Lives, and then caused the child to be brought forth, which in its Skin (not its Physiognomy) resembled a fair English Child.

From which last example we affirm, That 'tis more than barely probable that the first change of Colors in Persons came from such an instance as this; and where such an instance happened, *the news of its sight would form an Idea in others, which in the Act of generation would have the same Effect, the Imaginary power being stronger than the Generative, both in Women and other Creatures. We have frequent examples of the first, and want not some in the last, particularly in Jacob's policy of transferring Laban's Flocks into his:* (Genesis 30:37, 38 and 39.)

[37. Jacob, however, took fresh-cut branches from poplar, almond and plane tree, and made white stripes on them by peeling the bark and *exposing the white inner wood of the branches.*

38.Then he placed the peeled branches in all the watering troughs, so that they would be directly in front of the flocks when they came to drink. When the flocks were in heat and came to drink, they mated in front of the branches

39. *And they bore young that were streaked or speckled or spotted.]*

(emphasis is mine)

Now a color being once changed, it naturally follows that Intermarriages, Transplantations, and Commixtures of such Persons must have produced variety of colors, though we must allow a great cause in the nearness or distance of the sun.

The main questions that come to mind, if we were to accept this hypothesis are: why blackness in Lot's children should be seen negatively, and yet it was the only family found to be righteous in the two cities of Sodom and Gomorrah. Moreover, how does the change of color account for the physiological features like "kinky hair" and "flat nose?" If it could, *why would these features be seen as degenerative rather than evolutionary?*

As for Jacob's policy, is it scientifically proven? "No, what Jacob did would not influence the offspring of livestock. There is no connection between visual cues and genetic inheritance. The NIV Study Bible footnotes indicate that it was something special that God had to do, and then refers the reader to a verse in the following chapter". (Dr. Paul Rothrock, a botanist at Taylor University) There is no reason, therefore, to associate the smoke of Sodom with Lot's offspring. Moreover, no one can prove that black people are Lot's relatives.

With regard to the white child from two black parents there seems to be no explanation, except, perhaps that it was a miracle. Then why should the opposite not be possible, that two white parents miraculously had a black child, if humans were white to begin with? This, too has not been established without a doubt.

The distance from the sun was discussed further in Jordan. The question was if blacks who came to America would become white after living in a cold climate for a long time. Peter Kalm, who visited America, had the following to say on the topic: (Jordan, 243).

The Negroes have (therefore) been upwards of a hundred and thirty years in this country. As the winters here, especially in New England and New York, are as severe as our Swedish winter, I very carefully inquired whether the cold had not been observed to affect the color of the Negroes, and to change it, so that the third or fourth generation from the first that came hither became less black than their ancestors. But I was generally answered that there was not the slightest difference of color to be perceived. And that a negro born here of parents who were likewise born in this country, and whose ancestors both men and women had been all blacks born in this country, up to the third and the fourth generation, was not at all different in color from those negroes who were bought directly from Africa...but the union of a white man with a negro woman, or of a negro man with a white woman had an entirely different result.

I think it is, therefore, reasonable to conclude that the black color was then understood to be of genetic origin, perhaps part of evolution?

SECTION THREE: MYTHS BASED ON "PSEUDO" SCIENCE

CHAPTER 11

Evolution and "Scientific" Racism.

Conrad's <u>Heart of darkness</u>, considered to be one of the finest works of prose fiction in the English language, uses entry into Africa as a metaphor for entry into the dark heart of the human subconscious. As Marlow ascends the river (Congo) he experiences ever deeper human depravity until he finally reaches Kurtz, who lives among his own tribe of shouting cannibals with his sensuous African mistress. (to him going up the river) 'was like travelling back to the earliest beginnings of the world...we were wanderers on a prehistoric earth.'" (Keim, 38)

Keim continues to explain that the key to thinking about Africa as primitive, is the idea of evolution, in which primitive means "less evolved." Understood this way, all humans are not equal. "White human males of the upper socio-economic classes are at the very top of the human segment of the ladder. Others trail in a biological hierarchy constructed according to class, sex and race, known as the "chain of being." An example is given below from the website <http://jackytappet.tripod.com/chain.html> (accessed 0n 5/26/2011)

God
Angels
Kings/Queens
Archbishops
Dukes/Duchesses
Bishops
Marquises/Marchionesses
Earls/Countesses
Viscounts/Viscountesses
Barons/Baronesses
Abbots/Deacons
Knights/Local Officials
Ladies-in-Waiting
Priests/Monks
Squires
Pages
Messengers
Merchants/Shopkeepers
Tradesmen
Yeomen Farmers
Soldiers/Town Watch
Household Servants
Tennant Farmers
Shephards/Herders
Beggars
Actors
Thieves/Pirates
Gypsies
Animals
Birds
Worms
Plants
Rocks

According to another "Chain of Being" website, for centuries the 'great chain of being' held a central place in Western thought. This view saw the Universe as ordered in a linear sequence starting from the inanimate world of rocks. Plants came next, then animals, men, angels and, finally, God. It was very detailed with, for example, a ranking of human races; humans themselves ranked above apes above amphibians above fish. This view even predicted a world of invisible life in between the inanimate and the visible. Although advocates of evolution may have stripped it of its supernatural summit, this view is with us in the 21st century.

Another example is from <http://www.stanford.edu/class/engl174b/chain.html > 5/26/2011), is the great chain of being: a powerful visual metaphor for a divinely inspired universal hierarchy ranking all forms of higher and lower life; humans are represented by the male alone. (Didacas Valades, Rhetorica Christiana,1579).

The Great Chain of Being, as described by Aristotle, was adapted to the religious doctrine of Christianity through time to the early modern era, as describing the fixity of the natural world. The chain was later used to show how the ladder was fitted into the religious aspect of hierarchy as well as the political classes of humanity.

There have also been many critics of the great chain of being due to the fact that it contradicts people's religious beliefs. Problems for people with the great chain of being begin when it contradicts the biblical text, by stating that the world is over six thousand years old. Religious people also criticize evolution for the fact that the theory states that humans and monkeys came from a common ancestor. This posed a major problem for people of religion because it contradicts the biblical text that

Adam and Eve were the first beings on the planet. Religious constraints on the great chain of being became so stringent that evolution was not allowed to be taught in schools. However by the 1980s, creationists asked to present the scientific evidence against evolution: "the intelligent design theory."

Intelligent design refers to a scientific research program as well as a community of scientists, philosophers and other scholars who seek evidence of design in nature. The theory of intelligent design holds that certain features of the universe and of living things are best explained by an intelligent cause, not an undirected process such as natural selection. Through the study and analysis of a system's components, a design theorist is able to determine whether various natural structures are the product of chance, natural law, intelligent design, or some combination thereof. Such research is conducted by observing the types of information produced when intelligent agents act. Scientists then seek to find objects which have those same types of informational properties which we commonly know come from intelligence. Intelligent design has applied these scientific methods to detect design in irreducibly complex biological structures, the complex and specified information content in DNA, the life-sustaining physical architecture of the universe, and the geologically rapid origin. (Intelligent Design website).

On 12/21/2011 I watched a NOVA program that revisited Darwin's theory of evolution. The scientist explained that although Darwin knew that evolution takes place, he could not explain how it happens. Through the study of DNA, he claimed that now it is possible to see that there are two types of DNA, one that causes certain features, such as feet or hair to develop, and another that tells it to change. He gave the example of light skinned mice that move to dark colored rocks and their skins become dark to adapt to the new environment.

However, he said that those whose change DNA do not tell them to change die. The question is who or what decides who to be told and who not to be told? This would seem to me to be a case where an intelligent designer would be involved, because he does not want a certain species to continue, while he wants another to change and continue.

Unfortunately for the black people, by the end of the nineteenth century, the development of "Scientific Rationalism" had encouraged Westerners to believe that they had mastered "all secrets of the universe," including the inferiority of black people. Part of this was what came to be known as **"Scientific Racism."** Norton (2559) puts it this way:

> The enthusiasm for scientific discovery was not confined to scientists. Auguted Comte (1798-1857), a French philosopher known as the founder of "positivism," held that scientific method constituted a total world view in which everything would ultimately be explained, including human society. Comte proposed a science of humanity that would analyze and define the laws governing human society (the first sociology). It became evident, however *that the result of scientific method depended on the objectivity of the scientist's point of view.* (added emphasis)
>
> Count Gobineau (1816-1882) proposed a "scientific" description of society in which there were three races (White, Yellow and Black) with innate qualities and in which the white race (predictably, for this white man) was the superior category. Gobineau's writings laid the ground

work for much "scientific racism" later on, until he himself became the subject of analysis for scientists interested in explaining the history of race prejudice.

GOBINEAU'S THEORY

Gobineau's most important work, *Essay on the Inequality of Human Races* (1853-1855), partly translated into English in 1856, was an expression of his basic understanding of the meaning of his own life and of the events of his times. He was a royalist who despised democracy. He believed he was a descendant of a noble race of men, and he saw the French Revolution as a direct result of the bastardization of the race to which he belonged.

Gobineau sought to create a science of history by explaining the rise and fall of civilizations in terms of race. There were three races—the blacks, who were stupid and frivolous, but in whom the senses were well developed; the yellows, who craved mediocrity; and the whites, who were strong, intelligent, and handsome. Of the whites, the Aryans were superior, with the Germans being the purest of the Aryans. "German" did not refer to the entire German nation, *die Deutschen,* but rather to a tribe of Aryans, *die Germanen,* or Teutons, who had invaded Europe and set themselves up as an aristocracy to rule over the indigenous Celts and Slavs, who were inferior.

Gobineau did not believe that there are any modern pure races, nor was he set against all race mixing. He believed that civilization arose as the result of conquest by a superior race, virtually always Aryan, over inferior races. While Aryans were brave, strong, and intelligent, nevertheless they were a bit unimaginative and weak in sense perception. A small amount of infusion of black blood would heighten the senses and improve the imagination. Such an infusion, by way of Semites, explains the flowering of art and philosophy in ancient Greece.

However, Gobineau held that while some race mixing is good, too much is very bad, as it leads to the stagnation of civilization. Because Aryans have an appetite for race mixing, which made civilization possible in the first place, race mixing will eventually go too far, leading to the eventual destruction of civilization.

Gobineau was no nationalist. He associated nationalism with democracy and believed that both promoted excessive mixing of Aryan with inferior bloods. The disturbances of 1848 and 1871 increasingly convinced him that race mixing already had gone too far and European civilization was doomed.

RACISM AND EVOLUTIONISM

As we noted from Kipling's poem, the logic of evolutionism assumed that Africans were mentally equivalent to children and therefore, "could not produce art, religion, language, writing, literature or political structures that were as advanced as those of the west." (Keim, 43) for example, narrates how Schweinfurth described the Mangbetu people of the Congo as having "more European physical features such as lighter skins and longer noses," to explain their higher level of culture, and how they fitted the racial hierarchy as advanced savages.

In his book *The Mismeasure of Man*, Stephen Jay Gould chronicles the many attempts made to justify the Negro's inferiority through connecting the size of the brain to intelligence.

In the introduction (Gould, 21&23) he starts by stating that, "Science, since people must do it, is a socially embedded activity... Cultural influences have set up the assumptions about the mind, the body and the universe with which we begin; pose the questions we ask; influence the facts we seek; determine the interpretation we give to these facts; and direct our reaction to these interpretations and conclusions."

One of the ways the Negro was "proven" to be inferior by Morton, was to compare his head with that of a chimpanzee, as demonstrated in (Gould, 33). Through the study of the skulls (craniometry), Morton was able to rank the races. However, after a close examination of his final tabulations, Gould makes four conclusions: (Gould, 68&69)

1. Favorable inconsistencies and shifting criteria: Morton often chose to include or delete large subsamples in order to match group averages with prior expectations.
2. Subjectivity directed toward prior prejudice: Morton's measures with seed were sufficiently imprecise to permit a wide range of influence by subjective bias; later measures with shot, on the other hand, were repeatable, and presumably objective.
3. Procedural omissions that seem obvious to us: Morton was convinced that variation in skull size recorded differential, innate mental ability...Negroids yielded a lower average than Caucasians among his Egyptian skulls because the Negroid sample probably contained a higher percentage of smaller statured females, not because blacks are innately stupider.
4. Miscalculations and convenient omissions: All miscalculations and omissions that I have detected are in Morton's favor. He rounded the Negroid Egyptian average down to 79, rather than up to 80. (His averages for Germans and Anglo-saxons were rounded up).

Craniometry was further connected with Intelligence Quotient (IQ) by people like Alfred Binnet, the author of the Binet Scale, and again the black people were at a disadvantage. Binet's objective was noble, "to develop techniques for identifying those children whose lack of success in normal classrooms suggested the need for some form of special education," (Gould, 149). However, the results of his work were tragically misused. The main reason for this, according to (Gould, 155), was that people who used his scale ignored three cardinal principles for using his tests. "First, the score was meant to be a practical device for testing all children, but not to "define anything innate or permanent. Second, the scale was rough, not a device for ranking normal children. Third, the scores were to be used to identify children for help, not to mark children as innately incapable."

According to (Gould, 157) "American psychologists perverted Binet's intention and invented the hereditarian theory of IQ." An example was H.H. Goddard who used the IQ to identify the "moron." Finally the test was institutionalized nationally and associated, not just with intelligence, but any difference in culture between the Caucasian and other people, "the feeble-minded and the criminals." For example, Henry Fairfield Osborn (1923) is quoted in (Gould, 231) as saying, "We have learned once and for all that the Negro is not like us."

> Exceptionally prevalent in those whose faces are marked by developmental defects-by the round receding forehead, the protruding muzzle, the short and upturned nose, the thickened lips, which combine to give to the slum child's profile a negroid or almost simian outline...'Apes that are hardly anthropoid,' was the comment of one headmaster, who liked to sum up his cases in a phrase. (Gould, 281)

Other western disciplines worked out classifications
that connected African culture to biological inferiority.
For example, religious studies, psychology, art, science and
technology. The west associated technology with conquest of
nature and acquisition of wealth, so since the Africans did not
have machines, they were part of the nature to be conquered
and their knowledge was degraded. For example, Achebe in
"Racism in Literature…" argues that in <u>Heart of Darkness,</u>
Conrad characterizes Africans in a way that dehumanizes
them and sets up a contrast between civilized England and
uncivilized Africa.

This still goes on. For example, in 1994 while I was studying
at the University of Lancaster, a Kenyan colleague's dissertation
was questioned because she had used mainly oral sources
because there were very few written sources on the topic.
One would have thought that it was common knowledge that
most of the Kenyan languages did not have a writing system
up to the 1930s when Roman Catholic Fathers from Italy
created, for example, the *Gikuyu* orthography. Yet a system of
hieroglyphics existed long before any white man set foot in
Kenya, written on what was known as *Gichandi,* an instrument
passed on from one traditional historian (griot) to another.

Wangari Maathai, the late Kenyan Nobel prize winner,
describes the Gichandi this way:

> Before the arrival of the missionaries, Kikuyus and all
> the Kenyan communities had largely oral cultures. The
> ways they delivered a message or passed information
> included the use of drums, horns, shouting, or sending
> somebody. Among Kikuyus, one interesting form of
> message transmission and education was gichandi, which
> was made from a gourd. When you shook it, the beads on

strings on the outside and the seeds and stones inside made music. As players or actors shook the gourd, they relayed riddles, proverbs, and other folk wisdom and information. These gourds were also inscribed with symbols and marks that represented a form of writing that these artisans would use for recitations and conveying information.

Ironically, the missionaries described such instruments in detail, but then encouraged the local people who had converted to Christianity to destroy them. Even as they trivialized many aspects of the local culture, including various art forms, they also recorded them and saved some of the artifacts, which now reside in European museums. I have heard that one of these gichandi is in a museum in Turin, Italy. <http://hubpages.com/hub/Kikuyu-Scripts> accessed on 5/26/2011

One can only deduce that racism was a creation of the west to provide rationale for white dominance over people of color. It was further strengthened by the theory of evolution that suggested that western technology was the result of superior intelligence because the whites were more evolved, rather than the result of the necessity to exist in a hostile environment.

CHAPTER 12

Eugenics and the Human Genome Project

According to *Britannica Concise Encyclopedia,* eugenics is the study of human improvement by genetic means. The first thorough exposition of eugenics was made by Francis Galton, who in *Hereditary Genius* (1869) proposed that a system of arranged marriages between men of distinction and women of wealth would eventually produce a gifted race. The American Eugenics Society, founded in 1926, supported Galton's theories. U.S. eugenicists also supported restriction on immigration from nations with "inferior" stock, such as Italy, Greece, and countries of Eastern Europe, and argued for the sterilization of insane, retarded, and epileptic citizens. Sterilization laws were passed in more than half the states, and isolated instances of involuntary sterilization continued into the 1970s. The assumptions of eugenicists came under sharp criticism beginning in the 1930s and were discredited after the German Nazis used eugenics to support the extermination of Jews, blacks, and homosexuals.

The greatest influence in the sudden development of racism in the 19th century Europe was the replacement of the Christian belief that "God created all people equal" by "Darwinism". By suggesting that man had evolved from more primitive creatures, in short, Darwin is the father of racism. His theory was taken up and commented on by such 'official' founders of racism as Arthur Gobineau and Houston Stewart Chamberlain, and the racist ideology which emerged was then put into practice by the Nazis and other fascists. James Joll, who spent long years as a professor of history at universities such as Oxford, Stanford, and Harvard, explained the relationship between Darwinism and racism in his book <u>Europe Since 1870</u>, which is still taught as a textbook in some universities:

> Charles Darwin, the English naturalist whose books *On the Origin of Species*, published in 1859, and *The Descent of Man*, which followed in 1871, launched controversies which affected many branches of European thought...The ideas of Darwin, and of some of his contemporaries such as the English philosopher Herbert Spencer,...were rapidly applied to questions far removed from the immediate scientific ones...
>
> The element of Darwinism which appeared most applicable to the development of society was the belief that the excess of population over the means of support necessitated a constant struggle for survival in which it was the strongest or the 'fittest' who won. From this it was easy for some social thinkers to give a moral content to the notion of the fittest, so that the ***species or races which did survive were those morally entitled to do so.***

The doctrine of natural selection could, therefore, very easily become associated with another train of thought developed by, Count Gobineau, whom we discussed earlier. Gobineau insisted that the most important factor in development was race; and that those races which remained superior were those which kept their racial purity intact. Of these, according to Gobineau, it was the Aryan race which had survived best... It was Houston Stewart Chamberlain who contributed to carrying some of these ideas a stage further...Hitler himself admired the author (Chamberlain) sufficiently to visit him on his deathbed in 1927.

The evolutionist German biologist, Ernst Haeckel, is one of the most important of Nazism's spiritual fathers. Haeckel brought Darwin's theory to Germany, and prepared it as a program ready for the Nazis. From racists such as Arthur Gobineau and Houston Stewart Chamberlain, Hitler took over a politically-centered racism, and a biological one from Haeckel. Careful inspection will reveal that the inspiration behind all these racists came from Darwinism.

THE HUMAN GENOME PROJECT

According to the Human Genome website,

"Completed in 2003, the Human Genome Project (HGP) was a 13-year project coordinated by the U.S. Department of Energy and the National Institutes of Health. During the early years of the HGP, the Welcome Trust (U.K.) became a major partner; additional contributions came from Japan, France, Germany, China, and others.

Project goals were to:

- *identify* all the approximately 20,000-25,000 genes in human DNA,
- *determine* the sequences of the 3 billion chemical base pairs that make up human DNA,
- *store* this information in databases,
- *improve* tools for data analysis,
- *transfer* related technologies to the private sector, and

- *address* the ethical, legal, and social issues (ELSI) that may arise from the project.

According to the Human Genome website on Chromosomes, all the **human** chromosomes are the same, not grouped by race. This seems to suggest that all humans are essentially the same below the skin. Have the stories about different genetic makeup between whites and blacks been based on fact or prejudice?

Also according to the Human Genome website on minorities, DNA studies do not indicate that separate classifiable subspecies (races) exist within modern humans. While different genes for physical traits such as skin and hair color can be identified between individuals, no consistent patterns of genes across the human genome exist to distinguish one race from another. There also is no genetic basis for divisions of human ethnicity, but People who have lived in the same geographic region for many generations may have some alleles (one of two or more alternative forms of a gene) in common, alleles will be found in all members of one population and in no members of any other.

However concerns have ranged from the "fear of actuarial classifications of 'genetic exceptionalism' to the burden African Americans would face if they were among those labeled by some as a biological underclass," as earlier discussed. This may have arisen from discoveries that some diseases, such as sickle cell anemia have normally been associated mainly with African Americans. The new findings that other diseases such as cystic fibrosis are also mainly found among Caucasians should be used to show that this may be the result of something other than basic differences in genetics.

If all humans are more similar than they are different, how them can we continue the myth that black people are less than human, closer to monkeys than their white brothers? Moreover, it has been shown that blacks are as intelligent as whites, though this was hidden by the refusal to make African innovations public. This will be discussed further in another chapter.

One might argue that with the facts, we will know what to do. However, science cannot provide a basis for human judgment precisely because science can never provide all the facts.

SECTION FOUR: CONTINUING EFFECTS OF THE MYTHS

CHAPTER 13

Struck by Lightening: Loss of Self Identity

The fact that I am black had never been an issue, until I came to the US in the year 2001. I had always assumed that God had made me black, but had never considered the fact that the Bible says humans have a single set of parents, Adam and Eve. Were our original parents white or black? The question came about when I read and thought about black people who wanted to "whiten their skins."

In Kenya we have girls who use creams such as Ambi, though it is said to be dangerous because of its mercury content, but I thought they were just trying to remove pimples and create a smooth skin. When I read of men like President Obama, in his book *Dreams of My father*, and how he struggled with the idea of "passing as white," I realized the problem was serious. Whiteness has privileges!

Obama had started by distinguishing what the situation called for, comparing it to the fight against apartheid: "It's happening an ocean away. But it is a struggle that touches each and every one of us…A struggle that demands that we choose sides….between fairness and injustice. Between commitment

and indifference. A choice between right and wrong..."
(Obama,106)

Soon after, the <u>Jenda</u> Journal...called for papers on the topic calling it "the trans-diasporan phenomenon of skin bleaching." As I researched for the paper I read *Neither Black Nor White* by Carl N. Degler, a book that compares race relations between Brazil and the United States. He describes the race divisions in Brazil as follows, (105):

A "Negro" is anyone of the following:following:	A "white" is anyone of the
Poverty stricken white	White who is wealthy
Poverty stricken mulatto	White of average wealth
Poverty stricken Negro	White who is poor
Poor Negro	Wealthy mulatto
Negro of average wealth	Mulatto of average wealth
	Negro who is wealthy

He goes on to explain the two columns as follows:

Two conclusions stand out in this comparison of who is Negro and who is White. First to be of Negro ancestry is certainly a handicap; not as severe as of one in the United States, perhaps, but a handicap nonetheless. Second, as the Brazilians say, "money whitens," although it takes a good deal to whiten a full blooded Negro, even in Bahia. (Once "whitened" by money, a Negro becomes a "mulatto"or "pardo,"regardless of his actual color...One informant in Recife put the whitening process this way: When a black (preto) attains a prominent position-he has a ring on his finger. (The ring of a profession.) The black will be easily accepted.

From the foregoing quotation I began to realize why it may be advantageous for black people to bleach themselves, so that they can enter the privileged classes faster through what Degler refers to as the *"mulatto hatch."* This is the only way that seems open to black people to advance economically in Brazil. In the US, however, no such opportunity existed until recently. All people with even a drop of "black blood" were considered black until the election of Barack Obama as the first **black** (not Mulato) president of the United States.

Despite the president's open admission of his personal struggle with the race issue and a final decision that he wanted to be regarded as a black person, there was some discussion as to why his white heritage was being ignored. It seemed as if some mulattos would have liked to be thought different from blacks, thus giving them some advantage over other blacks. It will be interesting to see how the debate develops, especially since some black people said they would not elect him because he was "not black enough."

I also had another interesting conversation with a friend about a former Secretary of State in the US and how she used "the blush" as part of her makeup. My friend was shocked when I said I would never use it, since "blacks do not blush." She had never thought of it that way. This seemed to suggest that some bleaching may not be related to the idea of whitening for political reasons, but it may be seen as the way to be culturally accepted into the "sophisticated" class in a predominantly white society. But now we must return to political whitening in Brazil.

Speaking about interracial marriages, Degler says, (191):

Although in both the United States and Brazil there are and have been many examples of true affection as well as sexual exploitation in the liaisons between the races, the conclusion to be drawn from that history is not "that love breaks down barriers and unites human beings," but "that racial ideologies extend their conflicts even into love's embrace."

Of the obvious consequences of miscegenation, whether in or outside of marriage, is offspring of mixed bloods…in Brazil the children of a white and black couple are neither black nor white. This fact in itself encourages "whitening" by racial mixture. Indeed it has been argued that a national policy of Brazil is to have everyone eventually white, through the mixing of blood."

From these examples, one is forced to ask the hard question; how did the prejudice against black people arise and develop to the extent that blacks themselves have come to believe that they will never be good enough unless they are white? I shall attempt to answer this question from five main approaches: political, economic, religious, cultural and scientific, as discussed elsewhere in this book.

First, colonialism in the African Continent and slavery in the Diaspora, systematically trained the black person to hate his color and everything black. For example, when I was learning English at a school in Kenya, it was a crime to use my language (*Gikuyu*) anywhere in the school compound. The message was loud and clear, *"English is the language of the civilized and educated, Gikuyu is for the primitive and backward black people.*

I was also sent out of class by my missionary teachers on a regular basis for not combing my hair, although I did my best to comb my curly hair. Of course I got the message, *"unless you have blond straight hair, you are still backward and primitive.*" These messages remain with me still today. I especially remember them when my white students say they can't understand my "thick accent" or compliment me during winter when I have to wear a wig due to the cold, and tell me they like my new hair style. I have yet to be complimented when I have my "natural" hair!

Recently I used the term "natural hair" when speaking to my hair stylist and she was surprised, since she has always heard people talk about *"kinky African hair."* These are just a few examples of what colonialism did to erode our self-esteem as Black people and they are symptomatic of deeper psychological problems faced by black people.

Like colonialism, slavery went even further, as the following quotation demonstrates. Degler talks of the "Black mother on two continents" (170-171):

> ...one of the long rage consequences of slavery and racial discrimination in the United States was the disorganization of a large proportion of lower class Negro families...namely the absence of the father.

This leads us to the second factor; the black family has always been at the bottom of the economic ladder, both those in the continent as well as those in the Diaspora. Colonies were used mainly as sources for raw materials for the industries of the west, resulting in what African historians refer to as *"the rape of Africa."* This with the human exodus of more than 24 million slaves makes African countries some of the poorest in the world. After independence many of these countries have suffered from heavy debts to International Monetary Fund (IMF) and World Bank in form of Structural Adjustment Programs (SAPS).

Black people who are former slaves have had more than their share of poverty. For example, as I write, I hear from the media that more than 12% African Americans have lost their jobs, during the current recession as compared to half the number among whites. It is not difficult to infer that they had the less skilled jobs that were first to go as soon as the recession started, **in 2007?** Is it any wonder that blackness has come to be equated with poverty and backwardness while whiteness is equated with economic success? As I was finalizing this manuscript, it was announced that the Bank of America had discriminated against minorities, by steering them to the higher costing mortgages, which resulted in foreclosures. Racism is alive and well in 2011!

Religion, especially Christianity, is the third factor that has contributed to the low status of the black people. The story of Noah's son, Ham, has been used by some to explain why black people were used as slaves, as we discussed in section two. Tradition has been handed down that Canaan is the father of all black people, who were cursed to forever be slaves to their white brothers. Other passages from the Bible have also been used to strengthen this tradition, as we saw earlier. Closely following this is the fourth factor, the cultural prejudice that has been perpetuated through myths and racial jokes such as the ones Degler reports, and those in KKKomedy website, mentioned earlier.

Others have tried to explain how we became black, for example the idea of a second creation by Satan, alluded to in the last line of the poem. So, from these examples, we see the popular culture not just ridiculing blackness, but the body features and culture of the black people. Is it a wonder that many black men and women want to **escape** their dark skins? Notice, I have been talking about both men and women.

The fifth and last factor that I shall mention is science. During the Enlightenment period, scientists decided to create "scientific racism." This was a final consolidation of all the prejudices about color that had been going on throughout history. It was, like all the other "isms" of the time, supposed to be based on empirical research, especially a comparison of the size of brains of the three main races. It was decided that whites, especially of Aryan origin were superior to the yellows (those of Asian origin) and the blacks were at the bottom. I would guess this gave the Klu Klux Klan, and those who think like them, the license to fight for white supremacy and blacks the final blow to their self-image. This **"pseudo-science"** produced systems that have caused the greatest suffering to humankind: Apartheid, colonialism, slavery, and Nazism, as discussed in section one of this book.

EXAMPLES FROM DIFFERENT PARTS OF THE WORLD.

Merrick A. Andrew writes about Tamara, an 18 year old Jamaican girl, whose perception is that; "the fairer you are the more likely one is to become more successful, socially, economically and romantically." She points to the fact that the bleaching products are mainly made in North America and Europe and are often advertised using girls with "lighter" skin, names are constantly changed and the message is that "men do not like black girls." Some cannot afford these products so they use "tooth paste and curry powder." Her parents don't care what she does, but some girls, when challenged, say it is their bodies and they can do what they want with them.

Julie Masiga, a Kenyan, had the following to say on the topic:

(And) in keeping with international trends, here in Kenya the market for skin lightening agents has persisted. "You have to hold back the years," one woman says, "when I was young I would just wash my face and people would comment about (how) brown I was. Nowadays, I need to use something to even out my skin." Here 'even out' is a euphemism for 'bleach', as is the word 'fair' when used by manufacturers. But from one woman who looks upon light skin as a barrier to the aging process, to a young girl who believes that it is a mark of beauty.

Despite her chocolate brown good looks, Stella Mugendi is fully subscribed to the conventional standard of beauty, which dictates that light is right. "Guys don't notice you if you're dark, even if you're pretty," she says, "if I could make my skin lighter I would." And with some skin bleaching products retailing at as little as 10 shillings, she probably can. In fact, at that price, she is well within the group targeted by the local industry. To further illuminate this near obsession with light skin, are the comments from a former model who explains, "Men started looking for me from a very early age just because I am mixed and my skin is very light. They would say I looked like a mzungu," (means white person).

IS IT A "BLACK ONLY" PROBLEM?

A quick browse over the internet shows that white women also bleach their skins under the guise of "greater smoothness." Almost every Hollywood model uses some skin bleaching agent, thus making them a symbol for beauty and sophistication. So if black women are to compete for these positions, it seems to them they have to "bleach their skins."

It was shocking to me to see that now there are even "whitening pills." These are supposed not just to "bleach," but to make you "Younger." With all these "benefits," it seems to me the problem is here to stay. However, we cannot give up on our children. Just as problems in other areas, like medicine, have presented challenges that have been addressed aggressively, so we must continue to address this problem.

Akunyili, for example documents the process she used to deal with fake drugs in Nigeria, from which we learn how radical measures are necessary to deal with such grave problems. She starts by describing the use of a public enlightenment campaign thus:

> This is our most effective strategy involving dialogue, education and persuasion. It is sustained by using print and electronic media...in the major Nigeria(n) languages. Workshops, seminars and meetings have been conducted for most stakeholders. Mobilization campaigns for rural dwellers (are) ongoing.

In addition, she enumerates government actions to attack the problem from the source; the countries that "dump" these drugs, "for export only," that would not be allowed in their own countries because they tend to have a large dose of mercury and other substances that are too strong for even the black skin.

Finally, I think research exposing the harm done by the use of these bleaching products will help the users to make informed decisions. Parents and men, must be encouraged to participate, rather than make this a women's issue, which often happens. *It is a problem for the whole society.* Despite decades of humiliation, black people must learn to be proud of their values and their bodies, including their God-given dark skin.

CHAPTER 14

Poverty

IMPERIALIST RAPE OF AFRICA-AN EXAMPLE

Hochschild (page 70) describes Stanley's murderous descent into the Congo as documented in his own diaries. The King, (Leopold of Belgium) sent instructions to Stanley to "purchase as much land as you will be able to obtain, and that you should place successively under…suzerainty…as soon as possible and without losing one minute, all the chiefs from the mouth of the Congo to the Stanley falls…"

Companies operating in the Congo used prison stockades to keep hostages. If the men of the village resisted the demands for rubber it meant the death of their wife, child or chief. The Force Publique supplied military might under contract and each company had its own mercenaries.

Natives had to search out vines through inhospitable jungle. In Leopold's Congo it was an illegal offence to pay any Africans with money, so other more brutal forms of exhortation were employed. The British vice consul in 1899 gave a terrifying example of how the Force Publique carried out this task:

> An example of what is done was told me up the Ubangi [River]. This officer['s]…method…was to arrive in canoes

at a village, the inhabitants of which invariably bolted on their arrival; the soldiers were then landed, and commenced looting, taking all the chickens, grain etc, out of the houses; after this they attacked the natives until able to seize their women; these women were kept as hostages until the chief of the district brought in the required number of kilograms of rubber. The rubber having been brought, the women were sold back to their owners for a couple of goats apiece, and so he continued from village to village until the requisite amount of rubber had been collected. (Hochschild, 161)

An account in 1884 describes the actions of an officer, known as Fievez, taken against those who refused to collect rubber or failed to meet their quota: "I made war against them. One example was enough: a hundred heads cut off, and there have been plenty of supplies ever since. My goal is ultimately humanitarian. I killed a hundred people...but that allowed five hundred others to live." (Hochschild, 166)

Following tribal wars, state officials would see to it that the victors severed the hands of dead warriors. During expeditions, Force Publique soldiers were instructed to bring back a hand or head for each bullet fired, to make sure that none had been wasted or hidden for use in rebellions. A soldier with the chilling title "keeper of hands" accompanied each expedition. Force Publique soldiers were slaves who had been press-ganged through hostage taking, or stolen as children and brought up *in child colonies founded by the King and the Catholic Church.*

European and American readers, not comfortable acknowledging the genocidal scale of the killing in Africa at the turn of the century, have cast Heart of Darkness loose from its historical moorings…But Conrad himself wrote, 'Heart of Darkness is experience…pushed a little (and only very little) beyond the actual facts of the case."

It had been Conrad's boyhood dream to discover the heart of Africa—now that he had arrived he described what he found as *"the vilest scramble for loot that ever disfigured the history of human conscience." Conrad later added, "All Europe contributed to the making of Kurtz."* (143) Emphasis added

Leopold attempted to destroy the evidence: for eight days in 1908 furnaces in Leopold's Brussels headquarters were at full blast, as Congo State archives were tuned to ash. He sent word to his agent in the Congo to do likewise. This, the "politics of forgetting," was followed by the entire Belgian state.

The same story was repeated by the other colonial powers who looted everything, including land, raw materials and people, as cheap labor for their Plantations, such as the sugar plantations in the British West Indies. (Carrington, 167) describes the process as follows:

> Hiring enslaved labor varied from estate to estate and from colony to colony. However, certain features were common to all the islands. Slaves were hired on three main bases-some employed by the day, others by the job and still others on lease for varying periods of time, more than a year in some cases.

I have never been as shocked as I was the first time I visited the British Museum and saw whole walls that had come from caves in Egypt and artifacts of all types from other parts of

Africa and the world. Now people, including those from Africa have to pay to see these things.

THE BRETTON WOODS SYSTEM

According to Hill (344), the system was started in 1944 by 44 countries to replace the collapsed gold standard, during the Great Depression of the 1930s. The International Monetary Fund (IMF) to maintain order in international monetary systems, and World Bank to promote general economic development.

As the main custodian, the IMF had to use both discipline and flexibility. Heavy borrowers must "agree to monetary and fiscal conditions set down by the IMF." The system worked well until the late 1960s, but finally collapsed in 1973, partly due to the fact that only the US dollar could be converted into gold. A managed-floating system was introduced in 1976. It has, however, been criticized for its "one-size-fits-all policy," its moral hazard problem, (when people behave recklessly because they know they will be saved if things go wrong), and lack of accountability because it lacks the expertise to do a good job.

The effect of IMF in Africa has been seen by many as neo-colonialism, in which the west has continued to control Africa through "financial aid, by setting conditions that are not appropriate for the concerned countries. These countries have become more and more dependent on the west through high debt burdens that have crippled them to greater and greater poverty.

According to "The World Bank and IMF in Africa" website,

The U.S. holds roughly 17% of the vote in the World Bank and the 48 sub-Saharan African countries together have less than 9% of the votes. The Group of 7 rich countries (G-7) control 45% of World Bank votes. This system ensures that the World Bank and IMF act in the interest of the rich countries, promoting a model of economic growth (called neo-liberal) that benefits the richest countries and the international private sector.

On average, low income countries are subject to as many as 67 conditions per World Bank loan. African countries, in need of new loans have had no choice but to accept these conditions.

The World Bank and IMF have forced African countries to adopt "structural adjustment programs" (SAPs) and other measures which cut back government spending on basic services. They have required African governments to reduce trade barriers and open their markets, maintaining their economies as sources of cheap raw materials and cheap labor for multinational corporations.

As a result of World Bank and IMF policies, average economies in Africa have declined, and the continent's poverty has increased. Africa's debt crisis has worsened over the past two decades, as the failure of Word Bank and IMF intervention has left African countries more dependent than ever on new loans. These institutions have also undermined Africa's health through the policies they have imposed. Forced cutbacks in spending on health care, and the privatization of basic services, have left Africa's people more vulnerable to HIV/AIDS and other poverty-related diseases.

These problems have been discussed in great detail by a Zambian economist, Dambisa Moyo, and Jagdish Bhagwati, among others. For example, western governments accuse

African governments of corruption, which also occurs in the west, but in Africa for aid related reasons as well.

Arguments that aid can and should be used to promote development seem reasonable but have run into problems-not just because corrupt dictators divert aid for nefarious or selfish purposes but because even in reasonably democratic countries the provision of aid creates perverse incentives and unintended consequences, Bagwati (124).

All the government really needs to do is to court and cater to its foreign donors to stay in power. (Moyo- Wall Street Journal)

POVERTY RELATED TO SLAVERY

In addition to the fact that corrupt governments, like that of the late Saddam Husain have normally been in power through the support of western powers, until they stop "singing their song," and then they are toppled down, it is also a well documented fact that slaves were not allowed to learn how to read or write, and those who did were taught in secret.

They also did not own property for a long time even after the abolition of slavery, since the "forty acres and a mule" promise was not fulfilled. Many children of former slaves grow up in project housing and many of their men end up in prison. According to "States and Black Incarceration in America:"

US is *number one*, as we love to say, in incarceration of its citizens; we are only seconded by Russia. This means that the US has two million of its citizens in federal and state prisons and jails. And the gross unfairness of this system is that the vast majority of those in prisons are nonwhite citizens. That, of course, is no surprise; *we all know how criminal nonwhites are in America.*

Some interesting aspects of this study of prison statistics are these:

California, which has the sixth largest economy in the world, (including its Silicon Valley), and a population that is 52% nonwhite, and is supposedly on the cutting edge of racial and social tolerance, has a prison population that is 69% nonwhite. And, of course, with a Black population that is only 7%, it has a prison population that is 32% Black. And this large population of Black inmates has helped this enlightened state to be the sixth state in incarceration rates

Blacks also have a high rate of drop out from school, since many live in the inner cities with poor conditions and an early exposure to drugs. Consequently they have a very high rate of unemployment. For example, in May 2010 the rate of unemployment for whites was 24.4 while that for the blacks was 38, almost double, according to the US Department of Labor website. Many reasons contribute to this, but perhaps the most important is the *"achievement gap"* in education, as discussed in the next chapter of this book.

With such a poor start for blacks and the current view that affirmative action is "reverse discrimination," it is not rocket science to understand that black people are intended to, and will remain poor for a very long time. Some privileged younger generations of blacks have been convinced that there is equal opportunity and have come to look down on anything that tries to correct, rather than rewrite history, as is discussed in the last chapter.

In his book *The Coming Race Wars: A Cry for Reconciliation,* William Pannell describes other aspects that have contributed to the on-going poverty of the black people in the US. One thing that seems clear to outside observers, but now has been confirmed by this writer, is that white people are afraid, "afraid because they are white in a society that is becoming increasingly nonwhite," (Pannell, 81). "In sum, brewing in the nation is a full scale war of people groups against one another, and the issue is power. Powerless groups are beginning to realize that marginality in America is not about being **dumb**-*it is about being* **denied**...Those who have power are not about to give *it* away. Thus the only option for a powerless people is to take power away. How it is taken will be decided by those who have power. He goes on to illustrate this point by explaining the process of "white flight from the inner cities to the suburbs."

> White flight from cities is an old story, of course. It coincides with economic wellbeing. But it also coincides with government decisions to aid such movement with available loans. In a revealing piece on a changing America, *Business Week* chronicled the beginnings of the political process that developed the suburbs, and, in the aftermath, doomed the cities to decay. It began with New Deal attempts to get the economy back in shape after the Great Depression, one result of which was the gradual overcoming of puplic reluctance to accept government aid...they demanded that any "inharmonious racial or nationality groups" be excluded...the government policy made it impossible for black people and persons of other nationality groups to qualify. One black person in a block could result in having the loans cut off for the entire block." (Pannell 93/4)

This policy has had far reaching consequences for the inner cities, where most black people still live. Examples are the deterioration of the houses, poor schools and poor education, and violence. Also, "…twelve percent of the US population is black. (This population) owns less than a half of a percent of the total wealth of America. Our system has locked in the reward basically for people who have made it, and is preventing people who don't have anything but the shirt on their back from getting access to property and the seed corn and the capital and the jobs and the ownership of homes." (Pannell 95) Quoted in *Gentlemen's Quarterly, July,1992,p.154*. The same discrimination continues, as has been mentioned with regard to Bank of America's house loans to black people.

The problem of housing has continued today as many have lost their homes through fore closures. These too, have impacted the black community more because they are the ones with less education, and therefore less skilled jobs which were first to go during the current recession. Moreover, the little that might have benefited them with medical coverage, under what has come to be called, "Obamacare," is now threatened by the 2012 elections. The campaign, the development of the Tea Party movement and the 99ners, may be an indication that the class wars have already started. Yet many continue to point "holy" fingers to Egypt, Lebanon and Syria, as the places where human rights are violated. Are rights for black people "human" rights, one wonders.

As recently as the beginning of December, 2011, a white lady was interviewed on TV, whose church had refused to marry her. What was her crime? It was that of choosing a black husband. What kind of gospel do the members of that church preach, I asked myself? But then they are not the only ones. Many churches pretend that all people are welcome, until a black person goes there, and then their true colors become evident. Then one has the choice to leave or stick it out. I like to think of myself among the latter, or else I would always be on the move. After all it is no cliché that Sunday morning is the most segregated time in America. I used to think that black people are the ones who do not like white churches, but now I know it is a problem both groups need to think about, if they are to be true to the gospel of Jesus Christ, who died for all the people of the world. But perhaps I am only able to stay because I am a foreigner, and do not expect the respect for an American, who might see himself or herself being treated as a second class citizen.

CHAPTER 15

Loss of Black History

During my early schooling, we learned the history of the explorers like Henry Morton Stanley and David Livingstone who were supposed to have "discovered Africa." We never questioned what had happened before their arrival; we just memorized the dates in order to pass the Cambridge Examinations. However, when I went to the university, African professors made fun of the concept of "discovering Africa," saying that Africa did not come into being at the sight of the white man, but had been there many years. Could it be that it was Africa that discovered the white man?

In a recent article titled, "David Livingstone letter finally deciphered, " the author said:

> The university said the newly revealed letter projects an image at odds with the fearless hero depicted by Waller, who heavily sanitised Livingstone's writings before they were published posthumously.
>
> "It's an opportunity to rewrite history," said Harrison of Birkbeck, which announced the find. "It's giving us a new way of looking at Livingstone. He got depressed, he did

think he'd failed at times. But he never gave up...It makes him human.

This is just one example that illustrates the attitude towards the explorers as heroes who started history and African "natives" as those who had no existence before they were discovered. Yet we now know that the pyramids and the Great Zimbabwe, as well as many other marvels were built by Africans long before they set their eyes to a white man.

In an article titled "GREAT ZIMBABWE: A History Almost Forgotten," Professor Manu Ampim says:

The civilization of Great Zimbabwe was one of the most significant civilizations in the world during the Medieval period. European travelers from Germany, Portugal, and Britain were astonished to learn of this powerful African civilization in the interior of Southern Africa. The first European to visit Great Zimbabwe was a German geologist, Carl Mauch, in 1871. Like others before him, *Mauch refused to believe that indigenous Africans could have built such an extensive network of monuments made of granite stone.* Thus, Mauch assumed that the Great Zimbabwe monuments were created by biblical characters from the north: "I do not think that I am far wrong if I suppose that the ruin on the hill is a copy of Solomon's Temple on Mount Moriah and the building in the plain a copy of the palace where the Queen of Sheba lived during her visit to Solomon." *Mauch further stated that a "civilized [read: white] nation must once have lived there.* (Emphasis added)

In 1905, soon after Hall's destructive activity, British archeologist David Randall-MacIver studied the mud dwellings within the stone enclosures, and he became the first European researcher of the site to assert that the dwellings were "unquestionably African in every detail." After MacIver's assertion, which was almost equivalent to blasphemy to the British imperialists, archeologists were banned from the Zimbabwe site for almost 25 years!

It was in 1929 that British archeologist Gertrude Caton-Thompson led the first all-female excavation. Caton-Thompson investigated the site and was able to definitively argue in her work, *The Zimbabwe Culture: Ruins & Reactions* (1931), that the ruins were of African origin. She assessed the available archeological evidence (artifacts, nearby dwellings), and the oral tradition of the modern Shona-speaking people, and compared them to the ancient sites to determine the African foundation of Great Zimbabwe. Despite Caton-Thompson's conclusive evidence, the myth of a foreign origin of Great Zimbabwe continued for another half a century until Zimbabwe's independence in 1980.

After independence, President Mugambe summarized the intentions of the colonizers well: "Rhodes envisioned the British control of Africa from the Cape of Good Hope in the south to Cairo in the north, thus the slogan from "Cape to Cairo." His goal was to colonize the entire African continent and "to paint the [African] map [British] red." With such motives, the colonizers tried to erase anything that happened before their arrival in order to colonize the mind of the black person as incompetent and dependent on his master for survival.

It was equally important that the achievements of black people were not acknowledged in the lands where they had been taken as slaves. Consequently, whatever they did was credited to their masters, in case they got ideas in their heads that they were intellectually equal. One such example is found in "Life without black people" a humorous story about some white people who were so tired of living with black people that they wished them away. At first they were happy as they thought to themselves, "No more crimes, drugs, violence and welfare. All the blacks have gone."

Then suddenly they realized the New America was not the America they knew because so many things that had been invented by black people had also vanished. These included most crops that had been maintained by slaves, no skyscrapers because the elevators had been invented by a black man, very few cars because the gearshift, traffic signals were also invented by a black man and many other things. Finally they decided to have dinner in the midst of the chaos, but the food had spoiled, because a black man, John Standard, invented the refrigerator. For a more exhaustive list see "Museum of black inventions and innovations."

In his book <u>1001 Things Everyone Should Know About African American History,</u>

Jeffery C. Stewart discusses the many contributions black people in America have made to the society, most of which no one knows about. Under six main headings: Great Migrations, Civil Rights and Politics, African Americans in the Military, Culture and religion. Invention, science and Medicine, and finally Sports, he gives great details to demonstrate that this history has not been taught in the schools, thereby giving the impression that black people have never invented anything.

He notes, for example, that during the Civil war, at least sixteen African Americans received the Congressional Medal of Honor, "commendation established by Congress on July 12, 1862, to recognize enlisted men of the armed forces who 'distinguished themselves by their gallantry in action.'" (202-203) He also suggests some important books that those interested should read, such as *A Voice From the South* by Anna J. Cooper, *The Souls of Black Folk* by W.E. B. Du Bois, Collection of Black Art and others that try to fill this great gap.

Contrary to the general belief that blacks are only good in sports, as was recently expressed at my university by a student leader, Stewart demonstrates through 1001 examples that blacks have made a major contribution in all areas of life in America and the world. The student complained that the university was "buying" blacks for sports by providing scholarships, thereby lowering the academic standards because these sports men and women (most of them black) "were unable to contribute academically." This attitude is off course based on the idea that blacks are somewhat deficient intellectually. This idea culminates with the deficit models of education that have characterized black education, especially in the United States.

BLACK INVENTORS AND THEIR INVENTIONS LIST

almanac	Benjamin Banneker	Approx 1791
auto cut-off switch	Granville T. Woods	January 1, 1839
auto fishing devise	G. Cook	May 30, 1899
automatic gear shift	Richard Spikes	February 28, 1932
baby buggy	W.H. Richardson	June 18, 1899
bicycle frame	L.R. Johnson	October 10, 1899
biscuit cutter	A.P. Ashbourne	November 30, 1875

blood plasma bag	Charles Drew	Approx. 1945
cellular phone	Henry T. Sampson	July 6, 1971
chamber commode	T. Elkins	January 3, 1897
clothes dryer	G. T. Sampson	June 6, 1862
curtain rod	S. R. Scratton	November 30, 1889
curtain rod support	William S. Grant	August 4, 1896
door knob	O. Dorsey	December 10, 1878
door stop	O. Dorsey	December 10, 1878
dust pan	Lawrence P. Ray	August 3, 1897
egg beater	Willie Johnson	February 5, 1884
electric lampbulb	Lewis Latimer	March 21, 1882
elevator	Alexander Miles	October 11, 1867
eye protector	P. Johnson	November 2, 1880
fire escape ladder	J. W. Winters	May 7, 1878
fire extinguisher	T. Marshall	October 26, 1872
folding bed	L. C. Bailey	July 18, 1899
folding chair	Brody & Surgwar	June 11, 1889
fountain pen	W. B. Purvis	January 7, 1890
furniture caster	O. A. Fisher	1878
gas mask	Garrett Morgan	October 13, 1914
golf tee	T. Grant	December 12, 1899
guitar	Robert F. Flemming, Jr.	March 3, 1886
hair brush	Lydia O. Newman	November 15, 18—
hand stamp	Walter B. Purvis	February 27, 1883
horse shoe	J. Ricks	March 30, 1885
ice cream scooper	A. L. Cralle	February 2, 1897

improv. sugar making	Norbet Rillieux	December 10, 1846
insect-destroyer gun	A. C. Richard	February 28, 1899
ironing board	Sarah Boone	December 30, 1887
key chain	F. J. Loudin	January 9, 1894
lantern	Michael C. Harvey	August 19, 1884
lawn mower	L. A. Burr	May 19, 1889
lawn sprinkler	J. W. Smith	May 4, 1897
lemon squeezer	J. Thomas White	December 8, 1893
lock	W. A. Martin	July 23, 18—
lubricating cup	Ellijah McCoy	November 15, 1895
lunch pail	James Robinson	1887
mail box	Paul L. Downing	October 27, 1891
mop	Thomas W. Stewart	June 11, 1893
motor	Frederick M. Jones	June 27, 1939
peanut butter	George Washington Carver	1896
pencil sharpener	J. L. Love	November 23, 1897
phone transmitter	Granville T. Woods	December 2, 1884
record player arm	Joseph Hunger Dickenson	January 8, 1819
refrigerator	J. Standard	June 14, 1891
riding saddles	W. D. Davis	October 6, 1895
rolling pin	John W. Reed	1864
shampoo headrest	C. O. Bailiff	October 11, 1898
spark plug	Edmond Berger	February 2, 1839
stethoscope	Imhotep	Ancient Egypt
stove	T. A. Carrington	July 25, 1876
straightening comb	Madam C. J. Walker	Approx 1905

street sweeper	Charles B. Brooks	March 17, 1890
thermostat control	Frederick M. Jones	February 23, 1960
traffic light	Garrett Morgan	November 20, 1923
tricycle	M. A. Cherry	May 6, 1886
typewriter	Burridge & Marshman	April 7, 1885

CHAPTER 16

Racism and Deficit Models of Education

According to (Keim, 50), "Most Americans have learned to hide their race prejudices from public view." I have noticed the same at my university, where I will be accused of things like being aggressive or making grammatical mistakes, or even being disorganized, but the word African will never be used, although it is implied, just in case it is interpreted as racial discrimination, which is illegal. However, there are a few people who do not care, such as Stanley Burnham (1993), in his chapter on "Primitive Society in Africa," where he repeats the Dark Africa myths and concludes; **"cognitive deficiency"** was the cause of Africa's perceived backwardness. This is similar to the idea of the "African child" who never matures.

This idea of deficiency has been used to justify the **minority achievement gap**-the difference between the academic achievement of White, middle class students and their peers of other social, cultural backgrounds, especially African Americans, Latinos and Native Americans and has been explained in terms of **"genetic inferiority, cultural deprivation and difference, economic disadvantage and structural inequality."**

Genetic and cultural inferiority-The assumption behind these theories was that students' failure to achieve could be explained by their so called **"deficits,"** including their genetic makeup, poorly developed skills, and inadequate mothering, among others, (**Nieto, 91**). This reminds me of the colonial theory that Africans had a lower Intelligent Quotient (IQ) that was why they could not do as well as their white counterparts in international examinations. As discussed earlier, this came about due to the associations of brain size and culture, with intelligence.

These deficit theories were popularized by researchers such as Fank Reissman (1962), Carl Bereiter and Sigfried Engelmann (1966) and Arthur Jensen (1969). These have been criticized by William Ryan (1972, 61) and others, as "blaming the victims." However, they have persisted by **other names such as "at risk," and "disadvantaged" children.**

Economic and social Reproduction Theories were used to challenge "deficit" theories in the '70s by **suggesting that "structural inequality, racism and poverty could better explain poor academic achievement,"** (Nieto, 92). These theorists, such as Joel Spring (1972), Samuel Bowles and Gintis (1976) and Michael Kartz (1975), claimed that "schools reproduced the status quo, and not only reflected structural inequalities, based on class race and gender, but also helped to *create and maintain* these inequalities." Nieto, however points out that struggles such as those for bilingual education and for education of students with special needs were not accounted for by these theories.

Cultural incompatibility theory. According to this theory, **because school culture and home culture are often at odds, the result is a "cultural clash"** that gets in the way of student learning. Other names that have been used for this type of reasoning are "cultural compatibility, cultural congruence, cultural competence, cultural responsiveness, culturally relevant and culturally appropriate instruction," (Nieto, 93)

Gloria Ladson-Billings (1994), qtd. in Nieto, for example, coined the term *culturally relevant teaching,* **suggesting that "this kind of pedagogy is in sharp contrast with** *assimilationist teaching* **whose main purpose is to transmit the dominant culture's** beliefs and values in an uncritical way to all students." These theories assume that that teachers can learn to create environments in which all students can be successful learners.

SOCIO-CULTURAL EXPLANATIONS FOR SCHOOL ACHIEVEMENT.

According to (Nieto, 4):

Socio-cultural and socio-political perspectives are first and foremost based on the assumption that social relationships and political realities are at the heart of teaching and learning…The concepts are also highly consistent with a critical multicultural perspective, that is one that is broader than superficial additions to content or "holidays and heroes" approaches.

Middle class parents, for example, usually speak Standard English and they also tend to engage in school like pre-reading activities. Also there are different kinds of questions asked at home and school, and when teachers were made aware they asked more relevant questions that students could understand, and become more active participants (Heath, 1983).

Students as caste-like minorities. Popularized by (Ogbu, 1987), he suggested that in order to understand academic outcomes, it is necessary to look at a group's situation in the host society. **According to him, given the long history of discrimination and racism in the schools, involuntary minority children (those who came to the US by force) are often distrustful of the education system aka "the burden of acting White."** This may include such activities as speaking Standard English, listening to European classical music and even getting good grades. Instead they may choose to engage in "*oppositional behavior*" that defines their difference from the majority.

Resistance Theory adds to Ogbu's theory saying that, **"not learning what schools teach can be seen as a form of political resistance.** Erickson (1993) for example, maintains that whereas cultural differences may cause some initial school failures and understandings, it is only when they become entrenched over time that a consistent pattern of refusing to learn arises. The extreme form of rejecting education is **dropping out. Fine's (1991) research found out that the two major reasons for this are political resistance and disappointment with the promise of education.**

Kozol (182-3) describes some students he visited as follows:

> A teacher sitting with us says, "At eight years old, some of the boys are running drugs and holding money for the dealers. By 28, they're going to be dead…Four years from now, the principle says,…one third of the little girls…are going to be pregnant…I look into the

faces of these children. At this moment they seem full of hope and innocence and expectation...Two years from now, in junior high, there may be more toughness in their eyes, a look of lessened expectations and increased cynicism. By the time they are 14, a certain rawness and vulgarity may have set in. Many will be hostile and embittered at that time. Others will coarsen, partly the result of diet, partly self neglect and self dislike... Visitors who meet such girls in elementary school feel tenderness; by junior high, they feel more pity or alarm.

CARE, STUDENT ACHIEVEMENT, AND SOCIAL CAPITAL

Flores-Gonzalez (2002), in a study of Latino students in Chicago, concluded that **school structures and climate help create either "school kids" those who connect with school and have a chance to succeed, or "street kids," who have largely given up because they do not see it as a place where they belong.**

Stanton-Salazar (1997) also identified networks and institutional supports such as advocacy, role modeling, emotional and moral support; and advice and guidance through teachers and counselors, as factors that determine who makes it and who does not. This kind of support is linked to what Noddings (1992) called **"ethic of care,"** In this theory, whether and how teachers and schools care for students can make an immense difference in how students experience schooling. **This includes having high expectations and making rigorous demands.**

Racial and political ideology. Portes and Rumbaut (2001) in series of long term comprehensive studies of immigrant families concluded that the process of growing up as an immigrant in the US rages from smooth acceptance to traumatic confrontation. **Race can trump the influence of other factors, such as social class, religion or even language.** For example, immigrants fleeing from Communism are received more favorably than those fleeing economic exploitation. They cite Haitians, Nicaraguans and Mexicans as refugees whose earnings remain consistently low, while those of Vietnamese and Cubans, viewed as political refugees, increase each additional year of residence. For the former groups a college degree yields no improvement in earnings.

If these prejudices and perceived deficits against children of color are not addressed, especially through teacher training, allocation of resources and curriculum development, this discrimination is likely to continue for a very long time. (See Muchiri, Linguistic Challenges…)

CHAPTER 17

Disruption of Family Life and Culture

In "Bury my Bones..." The author explains: "the title of this article comes from a burial song by Onyango-Ogutu, a Luo writer and poet from Kenya, and represents its central argument, which is that a re-examination of oral tradition and its relation to modern written African literature is of crucial importance for African Literature."

The emphasis in the last few decades on the study of oral tradition has undoubtedly enlarged and enriched the field of literary study in general and African literature in particular. In her pioneering work, *Oral Literature in Africa,* Finnegan (1970:1), argues that the very notion of "oral literature" was unfamiliar to most Western scholars. She remarks:

> The concept of an oral literature is an unfamiliar one to most people brought up in cultures which, like those of contemporary Europe, lay stress on the idea of literacy and written tradition. In the popular view it seems to convey, on the one hand the idea of mystery, on the other that of crude and artistically undeveloped formulations.

However, "continental blacks as well as those in the Diaspora" have made great strides in recovering some of their cultures. For example, through folk narrative studies, people can learn things about the beliefs of their traditional ancestors. I did one such study of *Gikuyu proverbs* that has been reported in Muchiri *(Papers on Language and Culture...),* and found out that there were more negative things said about women than men. Another example is the work of historians who are interested in their origins, for example the "Roots" documentaries and other such studies.

Those interested in such studies believe that every culture should contribute to the common human wisdom that comes from their particular experiences. For example, although African Americans live in the same country as their white brothers and sisters, their experiences have been historically different. Trying to pretend to be someone else has never worked for anyone, even in today's so called global culture. It is becoming more and more obvious that there is really no "melting pot" of cultures, but rather "a mixing bowl." For example, I have been in the US for the last ten years and my culture is still essentially Kenyan.

Perhaps the aspect that was most affected by colonialism to a lesser degree and by slavery to a greater degree, was family life. In "Slave families" we read the following:

> Plantation owners in America had complete freedom to buy and sell slaves. State laws gave slave marriages no legal protection and in these transactions husbands could be separated from their wives and children from their mothers. In his autobiography, Frederick Douglas claimed that in the part of Maryland where he was born it was a common practice: "to part children from their mothers at

a very early age. Frequently, before the child has reached its twelfth month, its mother is taken from it, and hired out on some farm a considerable distance off."

The owner of Harriet Jacobs used the threat of selling her children as a means of controlling her behavior. In her book, *Incidents in the Life of a Slave Girl*, Jacobs described one mother, who had just witnessed seven of her children being sold at a slave-market: "She begged the trader to tell her where he intended to take them; this he refused to do. How could he, when he knew he would sell them, one by one, wherever he could command the highest price? I met that mother in the street, and her wild, haggard face lives to-day in my mind. She wrung her hands in anguish, and exclaimed, 'Gone! All gone! Why don't God kill me?' I had no words wherewith to comfort her."

It should be noted that the "divide and rule" principle was applied in both colonialism and slavery as the best method of breaking the spirit of the black person. It was not only the means for controlling the behavior of the individual person, but the group as well. With no intimate relationships there would be no real trust, and this would minimize slave rebellion.

The results have been devastating as many African American families are single parent families and many men have ended in state prisons. According to a new study from the Justice Policy Institute, a Washington, DC-based think-tank that advocates for alternatives to prison, "after two decades of harsh criminal justice policies, there are more black men in jail or prison than in college. At the end of 2000, 791,600 black men were behind bars and 603,032 were enrolled in colleges or universities. "

It is obvious that slavery is not the only cause for this problem, but is definitely a major contributor to the legacy of dysfunctional families among African Americans. In addition to this, the African Americans have to face what all Africans face, as expressed by Chinua Achebe, "All things Fall Apart." This came about as a result of adopting western culture because remaining African was equated to "savagery."

During the National Council of the Teachers of English (NCTE) centennial conference held in Chicago in November, 2011, Linda Darlington-Hammond, the author of *The Flat World and Education: How America's Commitment to Equity Will Determine Our Future,* made a strong research based argument that poverty and lack of equity among minority communities are among the most important contributing factors to the current low rating of the US system of education, (14th) among the developed countries of the world, like South Korea, Finland and even the UK. At a time when any politician who speaks of sensibly solving the immigration problem is silenced by being told he or she is declaring "an amnesty," for illegal immigrants, one wonders if this problem of equity will ever be resolved.

What these, so called patriots, forget is that when left behind, these children of minorities will drag the whole country down. Instead of just providing cheap labor for the millionaires, and sex objects for the morally deranged, they will also constitute disgruntled elements, which will not leave then in peace to enjoy their palatial houses in the segregated suburbs. Rich Kenyans live with this reality, despite stone walls and iron gates.

CHAPTER 18

Is There a Way Forward?

As some of you have read about these myths you must have wondered how people could construct such horrible things about black people from the Bible (especially the New Testament) the very book that talks about a creator who loves all people. I asked the same questions when I read about the passionate hatred by Moslems for Jews and Christians and (Nonie, 199-200) helped me to understand when she wrote:

> A(nother) reason for the silence is that for most Muslims, criticizing jihad, martyrdom, or terrorism seems in their minds-rightly or wrongly- to be equivalent to criticizing Islam itself." So they go on without doing anything about the wrongs with the attitude of *"wana mali"* (it is none of my business) and *"In Shallah"* (if Allah wills.)

Is it possible that some whites have kept quiet for the same reasons? Can we criticize the behavior of whites without criticizing the whole of the white race? The answer is "YES."

What about Christians, both black and white who stand and watch racism without lifting a finger? It is too dangerous to be involved in any attempt to change the STORY that one has heard since childhood. Most of these stories become part and parcel of who we are and changing them means changing ourselves, as Taylor notes in *Tell Me a Story*, (Taylor, 29)

> We tend not so much to use reason to construct our stories as to claim reasonableness for our stories after they have been formed. **Stories shape us first, then reason is used, by those who feel it necessary, to lend credibility to the views and values that the often undetected stories have given us…**but the underlying story is more important than the logical supports we can muster for it. We will cling to our story long after reason has wondered off.

Can we also dare criticize science? I shall leave you, my reader, to rationally consider what you have read and make your own decisions, **but remember the black person is not white, so asking him to be color blind is asking him to eradicate himself or herself.** Gwen Ifill, senior correspondent of Washington Week, summed it, in part, as follows when asked why she talks about President Obama's race:

> We have to find a way of speaking about race comfortably…as a positive thing. (When asked, can't we just forget about it? She says) I think that is silly. If you do not see my color, then you are not seeing me…My goal is not to use it as a deficit, to pull me back, to say I suffer somehow because of my color… We have an opportunity (to have a healthy discussion of race) that should not be squandered. (January 28, 2009)

Here are two cases currently being discussed, on which side would you be? Would your action help to rewrite or correct history? When we rewrite history we pretend that things did not happen, for example, some have said that the holocaust never happened; when we correct history we acknowledge that bad things happened, like slavery, but we determine that we shall never let such a thing happen again, because we are better informed, as human beings, than those who were there when those things happened. Unfortunately, slavery in the form of human trafficking is alive and well, but it is not politically correct to suggest that it is happening in America. Such things only happen in developing countries where there is corruption and where human rights are violated. These things do not happen in America!

WORLD CUP 2010 (SOUTH AFRICA)

A discussion was reported in the Wall Street Journal of June 28, 2010, of what was termed the "Dutch Question." Should descendants of colonists who brought Apartheid be applauded on the pitch by blacks who suffered greatly under their ancestors? A 28 year black South African, Melanie Grobbelaar said, "We're past all that." While Mr. Solomon, a 62 year old who was not even allowed to play in the white team during Apartheid, said, "It's my language and culture, also I like their style of play." What are the implications of such words?

Moreover, as recently demonstrated by the movie "Invictus," about South African rugby, soccer has also served as a racial bridge, just as baseball desegregated ahead of of America. That does not mean absence of dark memories for the blacks, for example Mr. Solomon said, "Of course, where the stadium is now. I remember there used to be a curfew horn at 8.45 p.m. telling all the colored they had to start heading home."

DORM THAT HONORS KLANSMAN SPARKS DEBATE (TEXAS, USA)

The University of Texas is discussing whether to rename a dormitory that for 55years has honored a late law professor and Ku Klux Klan leader. Those who oppose the change, for example, Dave Player, says, **"The University can't run from its own history, you can't wish away the transgressions of those who came before us."**

Supporting the change is Dr.Gregory Vincent who argues that the "University is pondering whether the dorm's name blemishes the school's reputation and compromises the public trust." Another member, Mr. Russell, argued that Professor Simkins was not simply a man who represented a prevalent racist view at the time, but rather a violent man who attacked newly freed slaves."

Whatever the decision on Simkins Residence Hall, Dr Vincent said that the University would use the controversy to educate the campus about UT's history. "No matter what happens," he said, "I do believe that we are going to use this as an educational opportunity of where UT is and where it was as a University."

Pannell, (135) in his concluding chapter discusses the role of the church by suggesting that three things must be faced, if progress is to be made in the issue of racism/tribalism: explore the "biblical concept of reconciliation," "be more clear about the meaning of spirituality, finally…explore all the avenues open to us for cooperation and partnerships across our metropolitan communities."

I believe these must not be left to the church, but must be the responsibility of all who want to make this a better place for their children, and avert the coming race wars. Maya Angelou (154) quotes Aime Cesaire's poem about the African: (reproduced below, in part);

My negritude is not a stone, its deafness hurled against
The clamor of the day;
My negritude is not a speck of dead water on the earth's
dead eye,
My negritude is neither tower nor cathedral...
It perforates opaque dejection with its upright patience.

In conclusion, I hope I have answered the question that sparked my quest: "Did God make the black person for humiliation and exploitation by others, as in colonialism, apartheid and slavery?" My answer is clearly, "NO!" This came about as a result of the STORIES passed on for over four hundred years, and that need to be changed. Change, however, is always difficult, especially when it involves power. Just as the Civil War in America and many national wars in Africa ended official slavery and colonialism, so must back people continue to fight the remaining racist stories, not by using guns, but by "decolonizing their minds," as one of my country men, Ngugi Wa Thiongo, has put it. As long as we accept the labels put on us, we shall remain victims of racism, but when we refuse to be hurt by them, they will no longer have power over us. Then we shall experience the freedom the Bible promises in (Galatians 3:13, 27):

Christ ransomed us from the curse of the law by becoming a curse for us, for it is written, 'Cursed is everyone who hangs on a tree... For all of you who were baptized into Christ have clothed yourselves with Christ. There is neither Jew nor Greek, there is neither slave nor free person, there is not male and female; for you are all one in Christ Jesus. And if you belong to Christ, then you are Abraham's descendant, heirs according to the promise.'

Works Cited

About The Klu Klax Klan

  <http://www.adl.org/learn/ext_us/kkk/default.asp?LEARN_
  Cat=Extremism&LEARN_SubCat=Extremism_in_
  America&xpicked=4&item=kkk> of 11-2-2011

Achebe, Chinua. "Racism in Literature: A Critical Essay"

  <http://www.bookrags.com/criticism/racism-in-literature-
  crit_10/>

Africans and Industrialization <http://countrystudies.us/ssouth-
  africa/15.htm>

Angelou, Maya Letters to My Daughter. Random House, 2008.

Aphartheid in South Africa From Day today

  <http://www.wordiq.com/definition/Apartheid#Apartheid_
  in_South_Africa_from_day_to_day> accessed 8-8-2011

Aphartheid, Reasons for <http://countrystudies.us/south-
  africa/15.htm>, accessed 8-8-2011

Apartheid, (Resistance)

  <http://www.english.emory.edu/Bahri/apart.html> accessed
  on 8-8-2011

Augustine, St. <http://www.augustinian.org/home>

Bergman, "The Origin of Creation Myths,"

<http://www.creationism.org/csshs/v06n2p10.htm> accessed July, 2011

Bhagwati, Jagdish. "Banned Aid: Why International Assistance Does Not alleviate Poverty." Foreign Affairs. Jan/Feb, 2010. Pgs. 120-125.

Black inventions and innovations

<http://blackinventions101.com/inventionslist.html> accessed in June, 2010.

Blacks and the priesthood/the "curse of Cain" and "curse of Ham"

"The biblical 'mark of Cain' associated with black skin by Protestants to justify slavery."

<http://en.fairmormon.org/Blacks_and_the_priesthood/ The_%22curse_of_Cain%22_and_%22curse_of_ Ham%22#When_did_a_biblical_curse_become_associated_ with_the_.22Hamites.3F.22> July, 2011.

Burnham, Stanley. Americas Bi-modal Crisis: Black Intelligence in White Society. 3rd Ed.

Athens: GA Foundations for Human Understanding, 1993.

"Bury my bones but keep my words: the interface between oral tradition and contemporary African writing."

<http://www.thefreelibrary.com/Bury+my+bones+but+ke ep+my+words:+the+interface+between+oral+tradition... -a0131356399> March 2011

Cagnolo, Fr. C. The Akikuyu: Their Customs, Traditions and Folklore. Mission Printing School. Nyeri, Kenya. 1933.

Carrington, Selwyn, H. H. The Sugar Industry and the Abolition of Slave Trade, 1175-1810 University of Florida Press, 2003.

Christian Churches of God, "Sons of Ham." <http://www.ccg.org/english/s/p045A.html>. February 2010

Chain of Being <http://hubpages.com/hub/Chain-of-Being> May 2011

"The Curse of Canaan" Return to Glory website: <http://www.freemaninstitute.com/RTGham.htm> March, 2011

Country Studies, South Africa: <http://countrystudies.us/south-africa/ >June, 2010.

Darwish, Nonie Now They Call Me Infidel: Why I Renounced Jihad for America, Israel and the war on Terror. Sentinel, 2006

Davenport, Marilyn (Obama as a child of a Chimp) <http://en.terra.com/latin-in-america/news/rep_davenport_depicts_president_obama_as_a_chimpanzee/hof14521/PPC=google_english&sem=1 > 8/30/2011.

David Livingstone Letter Finally Deciphered <http://www.3news.co.nz/David-Livingstone-letter-finally-deciphered/tabid/1160/articleID/164192/Default.aspx>

Degler, Carl N. Neither Black Nor White: Slavery and Race Relations in Brazil and the United States. Mcmillan, NY. 1971.

Dora Akunyili, "Women leadership In Emerging Democracy: My NAFDAC Experience" JENDA: A Journal of culture and African Women Studies: Issue 9, 2006.

"Dorm that Honors Klansman Sparks Debate" (Texas, USA) The Wall Street Journal
U.S. News, Monday, June 28, 2010.

Du Bois, W.E. B. The Souls of Black Folk, Norton and co.,1999

Dutch Reformed Churches: Rita M. Byrnes, ed. *South Africa: A Country Study.*
Washington: GPO for the Library of Congress, 1996.
<http://countrystudies.us/south-africa/>

Elkins, Caroline. "A Civilizing Mission in Late Colonial Kenya" From her book Imperial Reckoning: The Untold Story of the End of Empire in Kenya. Henry Holt, 2005.

Evenson, Darrick T. The Mormon Church and the Curse of Cain Legacy: What Mormon Leaders taught as Official Doctrine About "Negroes' for 130 years (1848-1778) and
How the Church is Trying to Cover- up Its Racist Past.
< http://markofcain.angelfire.com/ > July, 2011.

Free Republic < *http://www.freerepublic.com/focus/f-news/1072053/posts>*
Novembere 29, 2011

Galton, Francis. Hereditary Genius. Macmillan, 1869.

Gobineau's Theory < http://www.answers.com/topic/arthur-de-gobineau> 12-23-2011

Gould, Stephen Jay. The Mismeasure of Man. W. W.Norton and company, New York. 1981

Hill, Charles W.L. Global Business Today McGraw-Hill-Irwin, 2009.

The History of Apartheid in South Africa:

<http://www-cs-students.stanford.edu/~cale/cs201/apartheid. hist.html >April, 2010.

Hochschild, Adam. <u>King Leopold's Ghost—A story of greed, terror and heroism in colonial Africa</u> by Macmillan, 1998.

<http://www.wsws.org/articles/1999/sep1999/king-s06. shtml> January, 2011.

The Holocaust Revealed <www.holocaustrevealed.org September, 2011.

<u>The Holy Bible New International version</u>. Hodder and Stoughton, London, 1986.

How Europe Underdeveloped Africa

<http://www.novelguide.com/a/discover/aes_01/aes_01_00093. html and>

<http://www.marxists.org/subject/africa/rodney-walter/ how-europe/ch06.htm>

The Human Genome Project:

<http://www.ornl.gov/sci/techresources/Human_Genome/ home.shtml.>12-23-2011

<http://www.ornl.gov/sci/techresources/Human_Genome/ elsi/minorities.shtml>

<http://www.ornl.gov/sci/techresources/Human_Genome/ posters/chromosome/chromo21.shtml> July,2011

Intelligent Design <http://www.intelligentdesign.org/whatisid. php> 12-22-2011.

Jacobs, Harriet, <u>Incidents in the Life of a Slave Girl</u>

Jordan, Winthrop D. White over Black: American Attitudes Toward the Negro, 1550-1812. The Norton Library, N.Y. 1968.

Justice Policy Institute <http://www.justicepolicy.org>

Katongole, Emmanuel with Jonathan Wilson-Hartgrove. Mirror to the Church. Resurrecting Faith after Genocide in Rwanda. Zondervan,

Grand Rapids, 2009.

Keim, Curtis Mistaking Africa: Curiosities and Inventions of the American Mind. Westview Press, 1999.

KKKomedy <http://www.thebirdman.org/Index/Others/Othe rs-Doc-Jokes&OtherAmusements/+Doc-Jokes&OtherAm usements-Ethnic&Racial/NiggerJokes.htm> 12-22-2011

Life without black people <http://www.snopes.com/business/ origins/blackinv.asp > February, 2010.

Maathai, Wangari. Unbowed: A Memoir. Anchor Books. 2006

Mariscal, Jorge. Power Point Racism: How Military Recruiters Pitch to Latinos.

<http://www.chapman-immig.com/Articles/EssentialArticle53. htm>

Masiga, Julie < http://www.Africaspeaks.com/kenya 11082006. html>

"The Color Devide". Aug. 2006.

Merrick, A. Andrew <http://www.Jamaicans.com/Jamaica Primetime>

"The Mormon Church and Curse of Cain Legacy: Accessed on 3/30/2010

<http://markofcain.angelfire.com/>

Moyo, Dambisa. "Why Foreign Aid is Hurting Africa". <u>Wall Street Weekend Journal</u> March 21-22, 2009

Moy, <u>Dead Aid: Why Aid is Not Working and How There is a Better way for Africa.</u> Farrar, Strous and Giroux. 2009

Muchiri, Mary Nyambura. "Naming Systems in Africa" in <u>Papers on Language and Culture: An African Perspective.</u> AuthoHouse, Bloomington, IN. 2009.

Muchiri, "Women and land in Africa" in <u>Papers on Language and Culture...</u>

<u>Muchiri, Saved Through Fire: A Family experiences Kenya's War of Independence.</u>

Guardian Books. Ontario, Canada. 2004.

Muchiri, "Struck by Lightning" in Papers on Language and Culture...

Muchiri, "Linguistic Challenges in a Multilingual Set Up: Training Public Teachers for TESOL in Indiana, USA." Presented in Kenyatta University, Kenya, July, 2010. (To be published by Springer Press of Germany in 2012 in conference proceedings.

The Museum of black inventions <http://blackinventions101.com/inventionslist.html>

The National Alliance < http://www.adl.org/learn/ext_us/N_Alliance.asp> 12-23-2011

<u>The Norton Anthology World Masterpieces Expanded Edition in One Volume.</u> Maynard Mack General Editor, NY, 1997.

Obama, Barak, <u>Dreams from My Father: A story of race and Inheritance.</u> Crown Publishers, N.Y. 1995

Oden, Thomas C. How Africa Shaped the Christian Mind: Rediscovering the African Seedbed of Western Christianity. IVP Books (2007)

Orwell, George, Animal Farm, 1946.

Pannell, William. The Coming Race Wars? A Cry for Reconciliation. Zondervan Publishing House, Grand Rapidss, Michigan. 1993

"PowerPoint Racism: How Military Recruiters Pitch to Latinos"

<http://www.myspace.com/projectyano/blog/183608222>

Racism and Social Darwinism

<http://www.islamdenouncesantisemitism.com/thesocial.htm#dip>

"The Skin Bleaching Phenomenon"—Commentary by Merrick A. Andrew, September 2002

"Slave families"

<http://www.spartacus.schoolnet.co.uk/USASseparation.htm>

Southern Poverty Law Center

<http://www.splcenter.org/get-informed/news/us-hate-groups-top-1000>

States and Black Incarceration in America:

<http://www.gibbsmagazine.com/blacks_in_prisons.htm.>

Stewart, Jeffrey, C.

1001 Things Everyone Should Know About African American History

Main Street Books, 1998.

Sons of Ham: <http://www.ccg.org/english/s/p045A.html > March, 2011.

Washington, Booker T. <u>Up From Slavery</u> Dover Publication, NY. 1995.

Weary, Dolphus-and William HendricksI. <u>Ain't Coming Back.</u> Tyndale House Publishers, Inc. Wheaton, Illinois. 1997.

The World Bank and IMF in Africa

    <http://rainbowwarrior2005.wordpress.com/2008/11/07/ the-world-bank-and-imf-in-africa/ >

"World Cup 2010" <u>The Wall Street Journal.</u> Monday June 28, 2010

Would you like to see your manuscript become a book?

If you are interested in becoming a PublishAmerica author, please submit your manuscript for possible publication to us at:

acquisitions@publishamerica.com

You may also mail in your manuscript to:

**PublishAmerica
PO Box 151
Frederick, MD 21705**

We also offer free graphics for Children's Picture Books!

---

www.publishamerica.com

CPSIA information can be obtained at www.ICGtesting.com
Printed in the USA
LVOW050535010812

292300LV00001B/30/P